Meeting the French

PAM BOURGEOIS

KOLIBRI LANGUAGES

Acknowledgments

For this second book in the Practical Guides to Lifestyle, Manners and Language series, published by Kolibri Languages, my thanks are due, as always, to Kari Masson as Managing Editor. Her enthusiasm, encouragement and her excellent organisational and editing skills continue to be invaluable in getting everything into shape. I am particularly grateful for her support and belief in the project from the beginning.

Stephanie Hinderer as Artistic Director contributes greatly to the overall style of the series. Her great eye for detail, creativity and constructive comments are much appreciated.

I would like to thank Christine Comte for her very professional approach to the layout and page design of the Practical Guides. She has unending patience and her considerable experience as a graphic designer is a great asset.

My thanks, too, to Garth Lombard of Largemouth Frog Productions for his work on the audio recording and musical introduction and to the talented photographers who contributed to the visual appeal of this book.

I am also indebted to Erin Tremouilhac for her help in checking the facts, to Alison Tetlow for her thoughtful comments and to Jean-Marie Bel who read the draft copy and made several helpful suggestions.

Series Editor: Pam Bourgeois
Managing Editor: Kari Masson
Artistic Director: Stephanie Hinderer
Graphic Designer: Christine Comte

Contents

Foreword

"Enchanté!" What else could one possibly say upon meeting a French person? The French continue to enrich our senses in so many ways, inspiring the world with the deep complexity of their language and their inborn sense of beauty. In any given week, around the world, French writers – old and new – are quoted in the major international media. *Their* language helps us improve *our* language.

Words, for sure, but beauty too. A client cannot walk out of the busiest *pâtisserie* without the servers taking the time and trouble to tie up even the tiniest pastry with the prettiest little bow.

Let's add *exigence*. Yes, the French can be demanding. But, thank goodness for their "pickiness" – it has given us one of the great cuisines of the world and works of art that will never go out of the public eye.

To complement this output, it must also be noted that the French are great "receivers" too. Schooled from the youngest age on *l'esprit critique*, the French naturally analyze all commentary and every image around them. The French will absorb every word you say, and then begin what is truly their favorite sport: debating your ideas. And, most remarkably, they will sincerely and intensely give credit to multiple sides of an argument when they feel an opposing point has merit.

However, well beyond all the above desirable qualities, is the French concept of *amitié*. A term never used lightly, but once attributed, it is intended for life.

As so honestly illustrated in MEETING THE FRENCH, the readers will see that for their appreciation of beauty, their insistence on quality, their attachment to the people they meet, and their commitment to their language, the French have historically lifted us up and moved us forward. Next time you are in a French *café*, you will feel these qualities all around you. Prepare for this moment, then enjoy it – not everyone gets the opportunity.

Jane M. Robert
Chevalier de la Légion d'Honneur
President, Renaissance Française – USA
Former President, Federation of Alliances Françaises – USA

Part 1

INVITATIONS

L'apéritif

WHAT TO EXPECT

"Venez prendre l'apéritif." This informal invitation is a prelude to a convivial occasion or a relaxing time before the evening meal and is frequently the opportunity to get to know people better. As the invitation is often spontaneous, an *apéritif* has the advantage of requiring little preparation and of allowing the hosts to spend time with their guests without worrying about what is happening in the kitchen.

For French people, an invitation for an *apéritif* is not necessarily associated with an invitation for a meal. Chatting with an acquaintance can lead to a friendly suggestion to prolong the conversation over an *apéritif*. A new neighbour can be invited for an *apéritif* as a welcoming gesture without anyone feeling that they must spend the entire evening together. A group of colleagues can stop for an *apéritif* in a local *café* after leaving work, or friends can invite each other to their homes for an hour or so of conversation and exchange.

CULTURAL TIPS

Before drinking an *apéritif*, people clink glasses with each other. This is called *trinquer*. Usually they will accompany the gesture by saying *"Santé !"* meaning literally 'good health'; the complete expression is *"À votre santé !"*
Less formally, French people will say *"Tchin, tchin !"* which is equivalent to "Cheers!" On special occasions, people may wish you something specific instead, such as a good holiday or success in a job interview.

AN *APÉRITIF* HAS THE ADVANTAGE OF ALLOWING THE HOSTS TO SPEND TIME WITH THEIR GUESTS.

L'apéritif

Increasingly, the French will have an *apéritif* at home, with something to nibble, before their evening meal and then move directly to the main dish without a first course. As family meals become less elaborate and with both partners working, this maintains the importance of spending time together as a family while reducing the time spent cooking.

When invited by friends for a meal, an *apéritif* is served shortly after arrival. Usually the host will serve the drinks while the hostess sets out a selection of olives, nuts or small squares of crisp bread spread with pâté or a purée of crushed olives. Fruit juice is offered for those who prefer non-alcoholic drinks.

A restaurant meal also usually starts with an *apéritif*. As well as its original purpose of helping to stimulate the appetite, it also allows for a leisurely moment while deciding what to order or while waiting for the first course to be served.

◄) KEYWORDS

le verre	glass
un glaçon	ice
un biscuit à apéritif	aperitif crackers or biscuits
des chips	crisps, chips
des toasts	(small) pieces of crisp bread spread with something
des olives	olives
des cacahuètes	peanuts
du saucisson sec	cold, slicing sausage
un kir	white wine with blackcurrant liqueur
un kir royal	champagne with blackcurrant liqueur
un vin blanc	white wine
un muscat	sweet aperitif wine
un pastis	pastis
un porto	port
un apéritif sans alcool	aperitif without alcohol
prendre l'apéro	to have or to go for an aperitif
servir des apéritifs	to serve an aperitif
trinquer	to clink glasses
grignoter	to nibble

L'apéritif

CULTURAL TIPS

Although *l'apéritif* is the correct word, the shortened *l'apéro* is very commonly used in everyday speech. The full word would be used on a written invitation, or in a very formal context.

Port is served only as an *apéritif* in France and is not drunk after a meal or to accompany a blue cheese as in some other countries.

Apéritifs are usually served with olives, nuts, small pieces of toasted bread spread with an olive paste or other things to nibble on. These are collectively known as *des amuse-gueules*, literally 'something to amuse your face', *gueule* being a slang word for face or mouth. In restaurants, they are more politely called *les amuse-bouches*.

Apéritif time in the evening is usually around seven o'clock, or later if in a restaurant before the start of a meal.

If you are staying for a meal and have not finished your *apéritif* when your hostess invites you to the table, you can carry your *apéritif* to the table with you. However, you would be expected to finish it before starting your meal as it will not necessarily match your hostess's first course.

When invited for an *apéritif*, be careful not to overstay your welcome. About an hour is appropriate, as your French hosts will want to eat their evening meal afterwards. Of course, if your French hosts press you to stay longer, you can do so, but most invitations to an *apéro* are for occasions not intended to last too long.

More formal occasions, such as business meetings, conferences or presentations, will often finish with an *apéritif*. This can be a simple drink or an *apéritif dînatoire*. The latter will include an elaborate selection of delicate sandwiches, small glasses of creamed vegetables or fish, finger foods and a variety of small cakes. *Apéritifs dînatoires* are ideal occasions for people to move around and mingle rather than talking to just their neighbours at the table. They are also an opportunity for a company to invite and impress its clients.

As you travel around France, you will also find *apéritifs* that are anchored in the history of a particular region. It is always interesting to try these *apéritifs* as they are often made from local fruit or plants and frequently have a fascinating origin. *Absinthe* in the Jura mountains, *pastis* in Provence, *kir* in Burgundy or *pineau* in the Vendée all have an important role in local tradition. Enquiring about them can be an excellent way to start a conversation as you share the very French ritual of *l'apéritif*.

WHEN INVITED BY FRIENDS FOR A MEAL, AN *APÉRITIF* IS SERVED SHORTLY AFTER ARRIVAL.

 IDIOMS

- If somebody *boit une tasse*, he is not drinking a cup of tea, but swallowing a mouthful of water when swimming.
- Make sure people don't say that you *bois comme un trou*. It means you drink like a fish.
- *Boire un coup de trop* is to have one too many.
- *Ce n'est pas la mer à boire* means it's no big deal.

L'apéritif

HISTORY AND TRADITIONS

Drinks based on herbs, using alcohol to help extract and preserve their active properties, have existed in France since medieval times when they were used to cleanse the digestive system. Over time it became a custom to take these drinks before meals, as they were also thought to stimulate the appetite, and they came to be known as *apéritifs* from the Latin 'aperire', meaning to open. By the end of the 19th century, the drinking of *apéritifs* before meals had become very popular in France.

An early *apéritif* that quickly became famous was created by French chemist Joseph Dubonnet in 1846. His drink was based on wine and quinine and was invented to protect soldiers fighting in Africa from malaria. To hide the quinine's bitter taste, he added herbs and spices. When his wife served the drink to friends it became popular as a drink before meals. The *apéritif* called Dubonnet still exists today.

The habit of drinking *apéritifs* within the home, at all levels of society, became common in France after the Second World War. From then on, the *apéritif* came to signify not only a drink, but a convivial occasion when social contacts could be created or maintained. Increasingly, *apéritif* drinks were accompanied by olives or slices of *saucisson*, and then by special *apéritif* crackers or biscuits.

In a survey, more than 90% of French people said they enjoyed an *apéritif* at least once a week, preferably at home. It is a distinctive moment in the French way of life.

🔊 YOU WILL HEAR

— *Venez prendre l'apéro.*
Come and have an aperitif.
— *Je vous invite à prendre l'apéritif.*
I'd like to invite you for an aperitif.
— *Vous souhaitez un apéritif ?*
Would you like an aperitif?
— *Qu'est-ce que je vous sers comme apéritif ?*
What would you like for an aperitif?
— *Qu'est-ce que vous prenez ?*
What will you have?
— *Avec des glaçons ?*
With ice?
— *Je vous ajoute de l'eau ?*
Shall I add water?
— *Servez-vous en amuse-gueules.*
Help yourself to something to nibble on.
— *Faites tourner, s'il vous plaît.*
Pass it around, please.
— *Un petit peu plus ?*
A little more?

L'apéritif

CULTURAL TIPS

Pastis is a generic term for an anise-based drink. Many *pastis*-drinkers will have a preferred brand, so when choosing it as an *apéritif*, particularly when ordering in a *café*, they will often refer to the drink by the name of the brand they prefer. In the south of France, you may also hear people referring to it as *un jaune* because of its distinctive yellow colour.

Dressing for an *apéritif* depends on the nature of the invitation. If the *apéritif* is arranged in advance, you should prob- y change out of your jeans. However, if you overdress, it may look as if you are expecting to be invited to stay to dinner, too. For an impromptu *apéritif*, you can go as you are, although not in beachwear, unless the *apéritif* is at a campsite or on a beach.

🔊 LANGUAGE TIPS

If you're not sure of the French word for the drink you would like, you can always ask your host to tell you what he has by saying:
– *Qu'est-ce que vous avez ?*

Less formally, you could ask:
– *Alors, qu'est-ce que tu me proposes ?*

The waiter will probably suggest an *apéritif* when you are dining in a restaurant. If French friends have invited you and you are not sure whether they wish to order *apéritifs*, you can leave the decision to them by saying:
– *C'est comme vous voulez.*
It's up to you.

If you have invited French friends and want them to feel at ease to order an *apéritif*, you can say:
– *Oui, on va prendre un apéro n'est-ce pas ?*
Yes, we'll have an aperitif, won't we?

🔊 USEFUL PHRASES

– *Merci. C'est très gentil.*
  Thank you. That's very kind.
– *Oui, je veux bien, merci.*
  Yes, please. Thank you.
– *Je prendrai un porto, s'il vous plaît.*
  I'll have a glass of port, please.
– *Je préfère un whisky, mais sans glaçon.*
  I prefer a whisky, but no ice.
– *Un pastis, mais bien noyé, s'il vous plaît.*
  A pastis, but with a lot of water, please.
– *Vous avez quelque chose sans alcool ?*
  Do you have something non-alcoholic?
– *Merci, les olives sont très bonnes.*
  Thank you, the olives are very good.
– *Non, merci. Ça suffit.*
  No, thank you. That's enough.

L'apéritif

Remember

If French friends propose *une promenade apéritive*, they are suggesting a walk to work up an appetite.

The word *apéritif* can also be used to indicate the moment in the early evening when *apéritifs* would normally be drunk:
– *Ils sont arrivés à l'apéritif.*

When a French friend or neighbour invites you for an *apéritif*, it may be just a general statement of intent:
– *Il faut venir boire l'apéro un jour !*
You must come for an aperitif sometime.

When invited for an *apéritif*, there is no need to take a present for your hosts as you would if invited for a meal. Generally you would thank your hosts by inviting them for an *apéritif* in return.

It is necessary to come

ADVANCED USEFUL PHRASES

– *Il faut venir prendre l'apéritif chez nous un soir.*
You'll have to come and have an aperitif at our place one evening.

– *Ça vous dit d'aller prendre l'apéritif au café ?*
What about going to a café for an aperitif?

– *J'en prendrai bien un peu plus, merci.*
I'll have a little more, please.

– *Je peux vous proposer du whisky, du pastis, du kir ou du muscat.*
I've got whisky, pastis, kir or muscat.

– *Est-ce que vous auriez un jus de fruit, s'il vous plaît ?*
Do you have a fruit juice, please?

– *Vous pouvez m'ajouter un peu plus d'eau, s'il vous plaît ?*
Could you add a little more water, please?

– *Alors, aux vacances !*
Well, here's to the holidays!

– *C'est sympa tout ça.*
This is really great.

 **LEARN MORE**

You can find other examples of giving and accepting invitations in *Un séjour*, p.22.

You can refer to *Un mariage*, p.29 for further examples of thanking people.

L'apéritif

Most famous

Despite the 1914 ban on drinks with a high alcohol content – aimed particularly at *absinthe* – illegal drinks based on anise continued to be popular, particularly in the south of France. Paul Ricard, the son of a wine merchant, decided to openly sell an anise-flavoured drink, to which he added liquorice, and just pay the fines. After much lobbying, he was given permission to commercialise the drink officially in 1932. He called it *pastis* and it became an instant success. By the end of the 1930s it had become the best-selling *apéritif* in France.

Suze, based on gentian plants, was first sold in 1889 by Fernand Moureaux. Its famous slender, yellow-coloured bottle was included in a collage by Picasso in 1912. The origin of the name is disputed. Some think it referred to Moureaux's sister-in-law, Suzette, others to the river Suze in Switzerland.

Kir, a mixture of blackcurrant liqueur and a dry white wine, traditionally a burgundy *aligoté*, was named after Félix Kir, a canon and mayor of Dijon who allowed his name to be used in advertisements for the drink in 1952. When the blackcurrant liqueur is added to champagne, it is known as *un kir royal*, and when mixed with a red Burgundy wine, as *un communard*. There are many regional variations, all of which have continued to make *kir* one of the most popular *apéritifs* in France.

Quiz

Circle the words that don't belong.

A. *des olives, des noix, des pommes, des toasts*

B. *des glaçons, de l'eau, de la liqueur, du sucre*

C. *un verre à pied, un verre à moutarde, un verre à whisky, un verre à vin*

D. *un kir, un porto, un pastis, un tilleul*

E. *cracher, siroter, boire, déguster*

Answers: A. *les pommes* (apples are not served to nibble on), B. *du sucre* (sugar is not added to *apéritifs*), C. *un verre à moutarde* (not a glass for an *apéritif*), D. *un tilleul* (an infusion is not an *apéritif*), E. *cracher* (not a way of drinking).

KEY POINTS

L'apéritif...

- refers to the occasion as well as the drink.
- is not necessarily followed by an invitation to dinner.
- is a way of welcoming or keeping up with friends and neighbours.
- can be very relaxed or very formal.
- can be an opportunity to try a traditional local *apéritif* drink in many parts of France.

Le dîner

WHAT TO EXPECT

Being invited to a French person's house for dinner is a great opportunity to learn more about the French way of life.

Your hosts will normally make it clear whether it is a formal or informal occasion by telling you about other guests or whether the meal is to celebrate a special event. A spur-of-the-moment invitation may be *à la fortune du pot*, that is, something put together quickly. However, most occasions will be planned with the meal being the central part of the evening.

In France, you don't need to arrive on the dot. You will be expected to arrive about a quarter of an hour after the announced time. You should dress quite formally as a very relaxed style of dress may seem disrespectful. Similarly, if you don't know your hosts well, you should wait to see how they address you. Sometimes an invitation to people's homes is the occasion to move to a less formal relationship, but you should let your hosts take the lead and not be surprised if you are still addressed very formally as *Madame* or *Monsieur*.

CULTURAL TIPS

When you arrive at someone's house for a meal, you should greet your hosts and each of the other guests by shaking their hands. A general greeting to everybody already in the room is not sufficient. You should do the same upon leaving. Depending on how well you know each person, a kiss on the cheek may replace the handshake.

In France, it is important to comment on the food you are served. French people will talk about the presentation, the ingredients and the preparation and compare the dish to others they have eaten. Just a general remark at the end of the meal could make your hostess feel that you have not paid attention to the food she has prepared.

Le dîner

Don't expect a tour of the house when new friends or neighbours invite you for a meal. This is not common practice in France.

French children and teenagers are very used to sitting through long meals. They will, however, sometimes request permission to leave the table by asking: *Je peux sortir de table ?* They are usually called back to the table for the dessert.

You won't often find salt and pepper on the table in someone's home. It is assumed that your hostess will have seasoned the dishes appropriately and it would be rude to ask for more salt.

Once the *apéritif* is finished, your hostess will invite you to come and sit at the dining table. You will be placed around the table so that men and women alternate and couples are not sitting together. You will probably spend some time around the table as French meals are usually lengthy and unhurried, with time between the courses.

The table settings will consist of a large plate with a smaller plate on top for the first course. In some homes, the forks will be set with the back facing upwards. This comes from the tradition of ensuring that the hallmark is visible. There will not be a side plate for your bread, which is simply placed on the table near your plate.

ONCE THE *APÉRITIF* IS FINISHED, YOUR HOSTESS WILL INVITE YOU TO COME AND SIT AT THE DINING TABLE.

🔊 KEYWORDS

un verre	glass
une assiette	plate
une assiette creuse	soup bowl
les couverts	cutlery/flatware
un couteau	knife
une fourchette	fork
une cuiller/cuillère	spoon
une petite cuiller/cuillère	teaspoon
un plat	serving dish
un saladier	salad bowl
une nappe	tablecloth
une serviette (de table)	napkin
avoir quelqu'un à dîner	to have someone for dinner
dresser la table	to lay/set the table
mettre la table	to lay/set the table
mettre le couvert	to lay/set the table
passer à table	to move to the table
débarrasser la table	to clear the table
sortir de table	to leave the table
quitter la table	to leave the table

Le dîner

Conversation is usually lively and may, to the outsider, even appear too spirited. The French love debating and arguing, and politics will not be excluded from the conversation. Raised voices merely reflect this passion for discussion and are generally a sign that everyone is having a good time.

Guests are not expected to leave immediately after the meal is finished. Coffee will be served after dessert either at the table or in the living room and conversation will continue. So when invited for a meal in France, prepare yourself for good food, lively discussions and a fascinating experience.

Depending on how formal the meal is, there may well be a discussion between the guests and hostess as to whether the knives and forks or plates should be changed at each course. Guests will often say that it is not necessary, with the aim of reducing work for the hostess, but the hostess may insist.

It is very important to compliment your hostess regularly on the food. Contrary to some cultures, your hostess will accept compliments gracefully and not try to make light of her efforts.

🔊 IDIOMS

- *Qui dort dîne* means that he who sleeps forgets his hunger.
- *Il a toujours son couvert mis chez nous* means there's always a place for him at our table.
- *Cracher dans la soupe* is to bite the hand that feeds you.
- If someone is *très soupe au lait*, it means he or she flies off the handle easily.

Le dîner

FRENCH CHILDREN AND TEENAGERS ARE VERY USED TO SITTING THROUGH LONG MEALS.

HISTORY AND TRADITIONS

Le dîner used to refer to the first meal of the day, then the meal taken around midday. It was only in the early 19th century that it became used to refer to the evening meal. In some parts of the French-speaking world, notably Québec, it still refers to the midday meal.

Traditionally, the French ate their evening meal around eight o'clock. In rural areas, this allowed for the agricultural work to be finished, and in towns, for the journeys to and from work. It also allowed for the time needed to prepare the meal.

CULTURAL TIPS

When eating your bread, break off a small piece with your fingers rather than biting directly into the slice. Avoid cutting your lettuce, also. The leaves should be folded and eaten with your fork. If you are served *foie gras*, you should place small pieces of it on the bread that is served with it. You shouldn't crush or spread the *foie gras*.

It shows appreciation of a sauce if you clean your plate with bread when you have finished eating. In a family environment, a piece of bread held with the fingers is used, but to be really polite, the bread should be held on a fork.

When eating artichokes or asparagus with a vinaigrette sauce, place your plate at an angle, sloping it towards you and propped up on the back of your fork or spoon. This allows for the sauce to collect in the lower part of the plate and you can then dip the artichoke leaves or asparagus in the vinaigrette easily.

🔊 USEFUL PHRASES

— Tenez ! Je vous ai apporté le dessert.
Here you are. I've brought dessert.
— Je me mets là ?
Shall I sit here?
— Je me sers ?
Shall I serve myself?
— C'est très bon.
It's really good.
— J'aime beaucoup cette sauce.
I really like this sauce.
— Oui, je veux bien en reprendre un peu.
Please, I'd love a little more.
— Ce dessert est super !
This dessert is really good!
— Comment vous le faites ?
How do you make it?
— Merci de nous avoir invités.
Thank you for inviting us.
— Nous avons passé une très bonne soirée.
We've had a lovely evening.

Le dîner

Nowadays, the evening meal remains an important family moment. While less time is given to its preparation as many women work, dinner still usually involves all the family, with the exception of very young children, sitting down together and spending just less than an hour over their meal.

At weekends or when invited to the homes of friends or family, *le dîner* is even more important and usually lasts two hours or more.

WHEN SEATED AT THE TABLE, YOU SHOULD KEEP YOUR HANDS ON THE TABLE RATHER THAN ON YOUR LAP.

🔊 *Remember*

When people already have another engagement for dinner, they will refuse an invitation by saying:
– *J'ai déjà un dîner ce soir.*
I'm already booked for dinner.

Le souper is a more informal way of referring to the evening meal. In certain parts of France, if you know people well, they may suggest:
– *Vous restez souper ce soir ?*
Will you stay and eat with us this evening?

This comes from an old tradition in rural France of soaking a slice of bread in a stock or other hot liquid, or even red wine. Liquid served over bread was called *la soupe*, and over time, *le souper* came to mean the evening meal, and *souper* to eat it.

🔊 YOU WILL HEAR

– *C'est prêt. On va passer à table.*
It's ready. Let's move to the table.
– *Servez-vous en légumes.*
Help yourself to vegetables.
– *Je vous sers ?*
Shall I serve you?
– *Je vous laisse vous servir.*
Please help yourself.
– *Prenez de la sauce.*
Help yourself to sauce.
– *Un petit peu plus ?*
Would you like a little more?
– *J'espère que vous aimez.*
I hope you like it.
– *Je vais prendre les assiettes.*
I'll just collect the plates.
– *On va passer au dessert.*
We'll have dessert now.
– *Qui prend un café ?*
Who would like coffee?

Le dîner

CULTURAL TIPS

When seated at the table, you should keep your hands on the table rather than on your lap. Hold your fork in the left hand. To show you have finished eating, place your knife and fork at right angles on your plate.

Business lunches or dinners are nearly always in a restaurant rather than at someone's home. The French invite members of the family and close friends to their homes often, but generally invite business contacts to a more formal restaurant meal.

When invited for a meal, you should take a gift such as a bottle of wine, flowers or a dessert. If you choose to take a dessert, you should inform your hostess of your intention so she can plan her meal accordingly.

🔊 LANGUAGE TIPS

If you are worried about what to say to the person sitting next to you at table, you can prepare a few sentences beforehand such as:

– *Vous habitez près d'ici ?*
Do you live nearby?

– *Comment est-ce que vous connaissez Yvonne et Pierre ?*
How do you know Yvonne and Pierre?

– *Vous allez partir en vacances cet été ?*
Are you going away this summer?

– *Vous êtes allé en Angleterre ?*
Have you been to England?

You can also prepare a few phrases about yourself in advance. This will enable you to concentrate on what your neighbour at the table is saying rather than worrying about what you need to say.

🔊 ADVANCED USEFUL PHRASES

– *J'espère que ce dessert vous fera plaisir.*
I hope you'll like this dessert.
– *Où est-ce que je m'assois ?*
Where shall I sit?
– *Qu'est-ce que c'est joli !*
That looks really good!
– *Ça a beaucoup de goût.*
It's very tasty.
– *Vous nous avez fait quelque chose de très original.*
You've made us something really original.
– *Félicitations au chef !*
Congratulations to the chef!
– *Qu'est-ce que vous avez mis dedans ?*
What did you put in it?
– *Désolée, c'était très bon, mais je n'ai plus faim.*
I'm sorry, it's really good, but I couldn't eat anymore.
– *Merci pour cette excellente soirée et ce repas délicieux.*
Thank you for an excellent evening and a delicious meal.
– *La prochaine fois, il faut que vous veniez manger chez nous.*
Next time, you'll have to come and have a meal at our place.

 **LEARN MORE**

You can find further examples of thanking people in *L'apéritif*, p.8.

More examples of greetings, including when to kiss on the cheek, can be found in *Les rencontres informelles*, p.45.

Le dîner

Quiz

Fill in the blanks using the verbs below.
sortir, passer, reprendre, servir, vouloir, préparer

A. *Je vous _____ le pain ?*

B. *Vous voulez en _____ un petit peu ?*

C. *Je vous ai _____ votre dessert préféré.*

D. *Tu veux _____ de table ?*

E. *Je vous _____ ?*

F. *Vous _____ du café ou une infusion ?*

Answers: A. passe, B. reprendre, C. préparé, D. sortir, E. sers, F. voulez.

Most famous

There is a well-known film that most French people will know concerning an evening meal. Called *LE DÎNER DE CONS*, it came out in 1998 and was directed by Francis Veber who adapted it from a stage play he wrote. Its plot centres on a group of Parisian businessmen who hold weekly dinners. They each bring a guest they consider to be an idiot who they can ridicule. At the end of the meal they decide who has brought the dumbest guest. This comedy was very successful and won several awards.

The French singer Benabar had a successful song called *'Le dîner'* in 2005. It is a monologue addressed to his girlfriend saying that he doesn't want to go to her friends' apartment for dinner. He makes all sorts of excuses for not going, including the fact that there is a *"super bon film à la télé ce soir."*

KEY POINTS

Le dîner...

- starts with an *apéritif*.
- is a leisurely meal.
- involves talking about the food you are eating.
- is usually quite formal.
- is accompanied by lively conversation.

Un séjour

WHAT TO EXPECT

When French people take time off, they often stay, *faire un séjour*, with family and friends. City dwellers delight in visiting family members who live in the countryside as they consider they are returning to their roots, a very important concept for the French. Many French people have a second home or a holiday home, *une résidence secondaire*, which is usually *une maison de campagne*, a house in the country, to which they invite other members of their family. This means that an invitation to stay with a French family is a rare privilege as most free time is taken up by visits from the family.

If you are invited, you will probably find the stay more formal than in some other cultures. No helping yourself to food in the fridge, for example! On arrival, you will be shown your room, the bathroom and main living area, but wait to be invited before entering the kitchen or other rooms in the house.

CULTURAL TIPS

When invited to stay with a French family, you will want to take a present. Something from your own country will be appreciated and you can also take a plant or flowers. Just remember never to give chrysanthemums. These are associated with All Saints' Day, when French people buy chrysanthemums to put on the graves of family and friends.

Many families will not have an electric kettle, although these are now available in French shops. People generally boil water in a saucepan to make tea.

The children in the family will be called to greet you on your arrival. Politeness to guests is usually insisted upon and each child will greet you separately. Young children will expect you to kiss them and will proffer their cheek, as will adolescents. Remember to use the informal *tu* form when talking to them. Don't forget to change back to using the formal *vous* when addressing the parents, unless you have already been invited to say *tu* by the adults themselves. If the family dog greets you by jumping up, you will make everyone laugh if you use *vous* to an animal. It's just not done!

Un séjour

In the evening, make sure you kiss the children as they go off to bed and say goodnight to your hosts individually before going to bed yourself. When you see your hosts the following morning, don't forget to greet everybody individually again, either by shaking hands or with kisses as appropriate. A breezy "*bonjour*" to everybody at the breakfast table is not sufficient.

AN INVITATION TO STAY WITH A FRENCH FAMILY IS A RARE PRIVILEGE AS MOST FREE TIME IS TAKEN UP BY VISITS FROM THE FAMILY.

◀) KEYWORDS

le salon	living room/lounge
le séjour	living room/lounge
la salle à manger	dining room
la cuisine	kitchen
la chambre (à coucher)	bedroom
la salle de bain	bathroom
le canapé	sofa/settee
le fauteuil	armchair
le buffet	sideboard
le four	oven
l'évier	sink
le plan de travail	worktop/countertop
le placard	cupboard
le torchon	tea towel/dish towel
la table de nuit	bedside table/night stand
la table de chevet	bedside table/night stand
une armoire	wardrobe/closet
un dessus-de-lit	bedspread
une couverture	blanket
le potager	kitchen/vegetable garden
le portail	gate

Un séjour

CULTURAL TIPS

You will find some differences in appliances in French houses. Until very recently, all French washing machines were top-loading. The French didn't have extensive worktops or countertops in their kitchens and so there was no problem when opening the washing machine. As modern kitchens with large worktops are becoming popular, front-loading washing machines are gaining in popularity too.

When talking about a French house, you will often hear French people refer to its *exposition*. This refers to the direction the main rooms of the house face. A main room facing north is not considered to be *bien exposée*.

Family traditions are very important in France. Furniture that has been in the family for generations is often given a prominent place. Many French families will have an imposing linen cupboard, sideboard or wardrobe inherited from their great-grandparents. The size of such furniture is often a problem in modern housing with lower ceilings and smaller rooms, but the furniture is kept whenever possible. Even when buying new items, the French will often purchase imposing pieces of furniture in solid wood reminiscent of the old styles.

Your hosts will ensure you eat well and are introduced to regional specialities. Breakfast will be the simplest meal and will not be a cooked meal. Lunch and dinner will usually consist of a starter, main dish, cheese and dessert. Lunch will be served around noon to 12.30 and the evening meal around eight o'clock, probably with an *apéritif* just before. You will be expected to take your time over the meal, particularly in the evening.

French people are very proud of the region where they live and will be delighted to take you around or suggest where you should visit. If you make enthusiastic comments as you tour around, they will appreciate you as a guest, just as you, too, will undoubtedly enjoy your stay.

IDIOMS

- *Faire sa petite cuisine* means to do one's own thing.
- *Tirer la couverture à soi* is to take all the credit for something.
- If a man is *une armoire à glace,* it means he is built like a tank.
- *Mettre quelque chose au placard* is to shelve something or to put off until later.
- When there's a running battle going on between two people, you can say that *le torchon brûle entre eux.*

UN SÉJOUR IS AN INTRODUCTION TO THE FRENCH LIFESTYLE.

Un séjour

HISTORY AND TRADITIONS

Traditionally, French people did not spend a lot of time on the upkeep and appearance of their houses. As people from other countries, particularly the British, bought properties in the French countryside and made extensive repairs, the value of a house in the country increased greatly. This encouraged many French people to pay more attention to their houses, too, and as do-it-yourself and gardening stores spread, they began to spend far more time on repairing and improving their houses and caring for the surroundings.

The average country house used to be fairly basic inside, even when it was the permanent home. People would live mainly in the large kitchen area and spend much of their time inside seated around the kitchen table. The rooms were often quite dark as the windows were small to keep out the cold in winter and the hot sun in summer.

🔊 USEFUL PHRASES

– *Merci beaucoup pour votre invitation sympathique.*
  Thank you for your kind invitation.
– *Nous sommes ravis d'être là.*
  We're really pleased to be here.
– *La maison est très jolie.*
  Your house is lovely.
– *J'aime beaucoup la vue depuis la fenêtre dans la chambre.*
  I love the view from the bedroom window.
– *Le jardin est magnifique !*
  What a fantastic garden!
– *Je peux vous aider ?*
  Can I help you?
– *Où se trouve la salle de bain, s'il vous plaît ?*
  Where's the bathroom, please?
– *Nous avons très bien dormi.*
  We slept really well.
– *Vous avez des suggestions pour des visites ?*
  Do you have any suggestions for visits?
– *Nous avons passé un week-end très sympathique.*
  We've had a really nice weekend.

Un séjour

Since some of these houses were used only during the summer months, there was little comfort indoors, so people spent most of their time outside. Nowadays, there are both improved bathroom facilities and more comfortable interiors.

The introduction of subsidies from 1977 onwards for modernising or extending rural houses so as to accept paying guests also boosted the desire to make improvements. As the French began to develop a network of *gîtes*, or rented accommodation, in the countryside and convert parts of their homes so they could offer *chambres d'hôte*, a room with breakfast and sometimes the evening meal, the level of general comfort increased without the authentic characteristics of the houses being lost. The recognition and importance of a rural heritage that needs to be preserved is now well established.

CULTURAL TIPS

When you need to go to the toilet or use the restroom, you can ask for *les toilettes*. The French themselves have a series of euphemisms they use, sometimes humorously, such as *le petit coin*, the little corner. French children will say they are going to *faire pipi*.

City dwellers in France increasingly have cats and dogs as pets. In the countryside, these animals are still often kept for practical reasons and are not allowed into the house or treated as pets.

Do offer to help out when staying with a French family, but let your hostess tell you what she prefers you to do. It is not considered polite to insist by picking up the dirty dishes and going into the kitchen if you have not been invited into the kitchen.

🔊 YOU WILL HEAR

— *Vous avez trouvé facilement ?*
Did you find us easily?
— *Vous voulez de l'aide avec vos bagages ?*
Do you need help with your luggage?
— *Voici votre chambre.*
This is your bedroom.
— *J'espère que vous aurez tout ce qu'il vous faut.*
I hope you'll have everything you need.
— *Pour la salle de bain, c'est la deuxième porte à gauche.*
The bathroom is the second door on the left.
— *On va manger dehors sur la terrasse, si ça vous convient.*
We'll eat outside on the terrace if that's okay.
— *Demain, on fera un petit tour en ville. Ça vous va ?*
We'll go into town tomorrow. Would you like that?
— *Vous avez des choses spécifiques que vous voulez faire ?*
Is there anything special you want to do?
— *Vous avez bien dormi ?*
Did you sleep well?
— *Ça nous a fait vraiment plaisir de vous recevoir.*
We were really pleased to have you here.

Un séjour

🔊 LANGUAGE TIPS

When staying with a French family, it is often the simple, everyday words you will find you don't know. Before you set off, it's useful to think of all the objects in your own house and check that you know the words for the objects you are likely to refer to when staying with your French hosts.

If you don't know the word for something, you can always paraphrase:
– *Je ne connais pas le mot, mais la chose qu'on utilise pour essuyer la vaisselle.*
I don't know the word, but the thing you use to wipe the dishes.

You can also ask for the word by pointing to the object and saying:
– *Comment ça s'appelle ?*
What's it called?

🔊 *Remember*

Un canapé is the word for a sofa in French, but it can also mean an open sandwich, a small piece of bread with pureed olives or pâté on it, served as an *apéritif*. The context usually makes it clear which of the two meanings is the appropriate one!

When you want to show your appreciation of your surroundings, the presentation of the food or something you are shown, you can make a simple exclamation such as:
– *Que c'est beau !*
How pretty/beautiful/lovely!

Alternatively, you can show admiration by saying:
– *C'est très beau.*
It's really beautiful.

 **LEARN MORE**

You will find more examples of making appreciative comments in *Le dîner*, p.15.

For further examples asking questions, you can refer to *La politique*, p.75.

Un séjour

Most famous

Le Fort de Brégançon is an official state residence, used mainly by French presidents for their summer vacations. General de Gaulle organised the restoration of this medieval fortified castle built on a rocky outcrop a few metres off the Mediterranean coast, although he did not like staying there himself. All the succeeding French presidents have stayed there. Georges Pompidou liked it particularly, but François Mitterrand was not very fond of it.

Famous *séjours* include those of Napoléon who stayed at the Château de Fontainebleau on several occasions. His first visit was in 1803 when he was First Consul. He organised the restoration of the *château*, which had been destroyed during the Revolution, and stayed there as Emperor, with his court, on three occasions afterwards.

🔊 ADVANCED USEFUL PHRASES

– *Grâce à vos directions, nous avons trouvé sans problème.*
Thanks to your directions, we found it without any problem.

– *Votre maison a un très joli emplacement.*
Your house is very well situated.

– *Je vais vous aider à débarrasser la table, si vous voulez.*
I'll help you clear the table, if you'd like.

– *J'aime beaucoup cette armoire. Elle date de quelle époque ?*
I like this wardrobe. What period is it from?

– *Qu'est-ce que je peux faire pour vous aider ?*
What can I do to help?

– *Je peux vous donner un coup de main ?*
Can I give you a hand?

– *Nous sommes contents de faire ce que vous nous proposez.*
We're happy to do whatever you suggest.

– *Nous aimons beaucoup marcher si vous avez des promenades à nous suggérer.*
We like walking if you have any walks you can suggest.

– *Nous avons vraiment apprécié notre séjour chez vous.*
We really appreciated our stay with you.

– *Merci pour tout ce que vous nous avez fait visiter.*
Thank you for all the places you've taken us to.

tous les endroits où vous nous avez emmenés

Quiz

Match the first half of the sentence with its second half.

A.	*Vous avez fait...*	1.	*bien dormi.* F
B.	*Je peux vous donner...*	2.	*un très agréable week-end.* E
C.	*Votre maison est...*	3.	*bonne route ?* A
D.	*Vous habitez là depuis...*	4.	*un coup de main ?* B
E.	*Nous avons passé...*	5.	*très jolie.* C
F.	*J'ai...*	6.	*longtemps ?* D

Answers: A3, B4, C5, D6, E2, F1.

KEY POINTS

Un séjour in a French family is...

- a real sign of friendship and acceptance.
- a chance to practice speaking to children and adults using the right verb forms.
- an opportunity to discover regional food.
- an occasion to understand French notions of privacy.
- an introduction to the French lifestyle.

Un mariage

WHAT TO EXPECT

Passers-by stop to watch as cars decorated with tulle follow each other through the streets, accompanied by much hooting and honking of horns. If you are lucky enough to be invited to a French wedding, you will find it is quite an experience.

In France, a civil wedding is required by law, even if there is a religious ceremony. The mayor of the *commune*, the administrative district where one of the couple lives, is authorised to perform the ceremony. The wedding takes place in the *salle des mariages* in the town hall and is presided over by the mayor wearing his official sash.

The ceremony is short and involves the couple exchanging vows and rings and then signing the marriage register. If the couple has decided not to have a religious ceremony, the bride and groom will be photographed and feted as they leave the town hall, *la mairie*.

The religious ceremony, if desired, can take place only after the civil ceremony. It will be a longer service with the bride usually dressed in white and accompanied by bridesmaids. When the couple comes outside at the end of the ceremony, coloured confetti is thrown at them, although this is sometimes frowned upon and may even be forbidden.

CULTURAL TIPS

Before the wedding day, the future bride and groom celebrate the end – literally, in French, the burial – of their lives as single people. This is called *l'enterrement de vie de jeune fille* or *de garçon*. It used to be a meal held the evening before the wedding but is now usually held about a week before, often over a full day. It involves various silly tasks that the participants must perform.

On the morning of a French wedding, all the cars, including those of guests, are decorated with bows of tulle tied around the door handles and car radio antenna. Most people keep the bows on their cars long after the wedding for good luck, so you will see cars with somewhat dirty tulle bows as you travel around.

Un mariage

THE TRADITIONAL WEDDING DESSERT,
CALLED *UNE PIÈCE MONTÉE*.

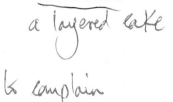

a layered cake

to complain

CULTURAL TIPS

For the civil wedding, both the bride and groom must each have a witness, *un témoin*. They will remain by the couple during the ceremony and will sign the marriage register.

If it rains during a French wedding you will hear people say, *"Mariage pluvieux, mariage heureux."* When it rains at a wedding, it is a happy marriage. In fact, the original proverb referred to a *"mariage plus vieux"*, meaning one where the couple was older and had more life experience.

After the wedding at the *mairie*, the couple is given *un livret de famille*, a passport-like document in which their names and the date and place of their wedding are recorded. The names and birthdates of any children will be added. It is an important document often required for administrative procedures.

🔊 IDIOMS

– *Faire un riche mariage* is to marry into money.
– *C'est le mariage de la carpe et du lapin* means they make an odd couple.
– *Se plaindre que la mariée est trop belle* is to object that everything is too good to be true.
– *On n'est pas mariés avec lui* means we don't owe him anything.

🔊 USEFUL PHRASES

– *La robe est très belle.*
   It's a very beautiful dress.
– *Vous faites un très beau couple.*
   You make a very handsome couple.
– *Félicitations à tous les deux.*
   Congratulations to you both.
– *Je suis une amie de la mariée.*
   I'm a friend of the bride's.
– *Tout était très bien organisé.*
   Everything was very well organised.
– *Le repas était très, très bon.*
   The meal was very good indeed.
– *Nous avons beaucoup apprécié cette journée.*
   We both really enjoyed today.
– *Merci de nous avoir invités.*
   Thank you for inviting us.

Un mariage

Although the people present will have received an invitation, a *faire-part*, informing them of the wedding and inviting them to the ceremony, they may not all be invited to the wedding meal. Usually there is a *vin d'honneur* held nearby where these guests will form a line to kiss and congratulate the couple and then have a glass of champagne. In some parts of France, some guests may receive a *faire-part* inviting them only to the dessert course of the wedding meal.

After the *vin d'honneur*, family members and the guests invited to the wedding meal will leave in their cars, hooting as they go, and make their way to the restaurant or hotel where the wedding celebrations are to be held.

IT USED TO BE TRADITIONAL TO THROW GRAINS OF RICE, A SYMBOL OF PROSPERITY AND FERTILITY, BUT THIS HAS NOW BEEN REPLACED BY THROWING CONFETTI.

◀)) KEYWORDS

un mariage	wedding
une alliance	wedding ring
la mariée	bride
le marié	groom
le témoin	witness
le faire-part de mariage	wedding announcement/invitation
la robe de mariée	wedding dress
la demoiselle d'honneur	bridesmaid
une église	church
la mairie	town hall
un(e) invité(e)	guest
un cadeau de mariage	wedding gift
la lune de miel	honeymoon
être invité à un mariage	to be invited to a wedding
féliciter les mariés	to congratulate the newly-weds
prendre des photos	to take photos
klaxonner	to hoot/honk one's horn
faire un cadeau	to give a present

Un mariage

The traditions of the wedding meal and the celebrations that follow it vary considerably from one region of France to another. In all regions though, the meal will be elaborate with several courses, often including *des trous normands*, literally Normandy holes, when either glasses of liqueurs, or more commonly nowadays sorbets made with liqueurs, usually Calvados, are served between the main courses to help with the digestion.

The wedding celebrations will often continue the following day and if the bride and groom are leaving on a honeymoon, *une lune de miel*, it will often be a couple of days later.

A wedding is one of the biggest family celebrations in France. It results in lots of photos that the extended French family will pass around and display with pride.

CULTURAL TIPS

In France, both men and women usually have a wedding ring. They are worn on the left hand and there is a preference for white gold over yellow gold. The bands are usually simple in design.

Guests wishing to give a present to the newly-weds can chose from a list of gifts in a selected shop. Sometimes, rather than *une liste de marriage*, *une cagnotte*, a collection of money, placed in a special box during the wedding celebrations, is preferred.

In traditional weddings, the bride may wear a special garter with ribbons, *une jarretière*. It is usually blue and white to symbolise purity and faithfulness. During the wedding meal, it is removed and sold to the highest bidder and the money given to the couple.

🔊 YOU WILL HEAR

– *Vous êtes du côté de la mariée ou du marié ?*
Are you on the bride's or the groom's side?
– *Tout le monde est invité à se mettre sur les marches de la mairie pour les photos.*
Everyone on the steps of the town hall for the photos, please.
– *Nous allons remonter dans les voitures pour aller au restaurant.*
We're going to take the cars to go to the restaurant.
– *Vous êtes priés de prendre votre place à table.*
Please take your place at the table.
– *Nous allons trinquer à la santé des mariés.*
We're going to drink to the good health of the newly-weds.
– *Nous allons débarrasser les tables pour pouvoir danser.*
We're going to clear the tables so we can dance.
– *Votre cadeau a été très apprécié.*
We really liked your present.
– *Merci d'être venu.*
Thank you for coming.

Un mariage

HISTORY AND TRADITIONS

It was in 1215 that the Catholic Church in France instituted stricter rules for weddings and made the wedding ceremony a sacrament. Banns, the notice given of an intended marriage, had to be published prior to the ceremony and both bride and groom had to say out loud that they consented to the wedding. In 1563, the *Concile de Trente* strengthened the role of the church further. The wedding had to take place before a priest with two witnesses who each signed the register. Living together outside of wedlock was forbidden.

In 1792, after the French Revolution, the state incorporated many of these aspects into the civil wedding that became the only marriage ceremony that was legally valid. In 1804, Napoleon's Civil Code further defined the rules for weddings with the legal ceremony being conducted by the mayor and not a priest.

In the 20th century, the vows were modified so that the husband no longer had to promise to protect his wife and the wife no longer promised obedience to her husband.

In France today, many couples do not marry, preferring a civil contract, *le Pacte civil de solidarité*, referred to as *le Pacs*. A couple is then said to be *pacsé* rather than married.

🔊 ADVANCED USEFUL PHRASES

– *Nous sommes ravis d'être invités au mariage de votre fils.*
   We are delighted to be invited to your son's wedding.
– *Vous pouvez m'expliquer dans quel ordre se passeront les choses ?*
   Can you tell me in what order things will be happening?
– *Est-ce que le mariage sera à l'église ou uniquement à la mairie ?*
   Will the wedding be in a church or at the town hall only?
– *Combien d'invités y aura-t-il ?*
   How many guests will there be ?
– *Comment faut-il s'habiller pour le mariage ?*
   How should I dress for the wedding?
– *Quel cadeau ferait plaisir à votre fille ?*
   Is there something your daughter would like as a present?
– *À quelle heure voulez-vous qu'on vienne ?*
   When should we arrive?
– *Est-ce qu'il y a quelque chose que je pourrais faire pour vous aider ?*
   Is there anything I can do to help?

🔊 *Remember*

In French, the same word is used for both the institution of marriage and the wedding ceremony itself. So you can say :
– *Au début de leur mariage, ils habitaient à Paris.*
When they were first married, they lived in Paris.
– *Le mariage a lieu ce samedi.*
The wedding is on Saturday.

When you want to say that Jean has married Renée, you need to use the verb *épouser*, which means to marry or to wed.
– *Jean a épousé Renée.*

You can use the verb *marier* when you want to say that Yves has married his daughter to a doctor.
– *Yves a marié sa fille à un médecin.*

Remember that *se marier* also means to harmonize :
– *Le noir se marie très bien avec le rouge.*
Black goes very well with red.

Un mariage

AFTER THE *VIN D'HONNEUR*, FAMILY MEMBERS AND THE GUESTS INVITED TO THE WEDDING MEAL WILL LEAVE IN THEIR CARS, HOOTING AS THEY GO, AND MAKE THEIR WAY TO THE WEDDING CELEBRATIONS.

🔊 LANGUAGE TIPS

Before going to a wedding, you can prepare the words to describe the different family relationships. On these occasions it's always useful to be able to ask another guest:

– *C'est qui le monsieur avec les cheveux gris ?*
Who's the gentleman with the grey hair?

Then, you will understand when you are told the person is:
– *C'est le grand-père de la mariée.*
He's the bride's grandfather.

– *C'est le beau-père de la sœur du marié.*
He's the groom's sister's father-in-law.

– *C'est le neveu du témoin du marié.*
He's the nephew of the groom's best man.

You should also be able to introduce yourself:
– *Je suis une amie de la mère de la mariée.*
I'm a friend of the bride's mother.

CULTURAL TIPS

The traditional wedding dessert, called *une pièce montée*, is a cake made of caramelised balls of choux pastry, filled with confectioner's cream and piled high on top of each other in a pyramid shape. It is extremely difficult to cut without the whole thing coming apart!

In the Vendée region of France, the dessert is an enormous *brioche* placed on a wooden tray with poles at the corners. To signal the start of the dancing, the bride and groom must circle carrying the *brioche* over their heads. Family and friends take over until finally the *brioche* is lowered and cut into pieces for the guests to eat.

 **LEARN MORE**

There are further examples of asking for more information in *Les différences régionales*, p.59.

For other terms describing family relationships, you can refer to *La famille*, p.52.

Un mariage

Most famous

Some well-known traditions associated with French weddings have gradually died out. It used to be traditional to throw grains of rice, a symbol of prosperity and fertility, at the couple as they came out of the civil or religious ceremony, but this has now been replaced by throwing confetti.

After the wedding meal and the dancing, the couple used to be accompanied to wherever they were staying by guests making a lot of noise. They would previously have put the room in disarray. In other regions of France, the couple would slip away discreetly from the wedding celebrations, then, early the next morning, some of the guests would set out to find them, knocking on all the doors in the village. They would carry a large chamber pot with them from which they would make the newly-weds drink once they had found them.

In other regions, a wooden box containing bottles of good wine is buried. It is dug up to celebrate the birth of the first child.

As guests leave the wedding, they are traditionally given a little packet of *dragées*, sugar-coated almonds as a symbol of eternal love and fertility.

KEY POINTS

Un mariage...

- requires a civil ceremony to be recognised.
- may involve an invitation for part of the occasion only.
- is followed by an elaborate meal and dancing.
- can have different customs depending on the region.
- usually includes a procession of cars and much hooting of horns.

Are the following statements true or false?

A. In France, couples must have a civil wedding even if they have a religious ceremony.
☑ True ☐ False

B. If you receive a *faire-part* for a wedding, it means you are invited to the wedding meal.
☑ True ☑ False

C. Both the bride and groom must have witnesses for the civil wedding.
☑ True ☐ False

D. *Une pièce montée* is the traditional main course at a wedding meal.
☐ True ☑ False

E. *Un livret de famille* is given to each of the newlyweds.
☐ True ☑ False

F. In France, couples leave for their honeymoon on the evening of their wedding.
☐ True ☑ False

Answers: A. True, B. False, C. True, D. False, E. False, F. False.

As they say in French

- « *L'apéritif, c'est la prière du soir des Français.* »
  Paul Morand

- « *La table est l'entremetteuse de l'amitié.* »
  Proverbe français

- « *La table est le plus sûr thermomètre de la fortune dans les ménages parisiens.* »
  Honoré de Balzac

- « *Le mariage, c'est l'art pour deux personnes de vivre ensemble aussi heureuses qu'elles auraient vécu chacune de leur côté.* »
  Georges Feydeau

- « *Un bon mari ne se souvient jamais de l'âge de sa femme, mais de son anniversaire, toujours.* »
  Jacques Audiberti

- « *Un mois avant le mariage, il parle, elle écoute. Un mois après le mariage, elle parle, il écoute. Dix ans après le mariage, ils parlent en même temps et les voisins écoutent.* »
  Pierre Véron

Part 2

MEETING PEOPLE

Les rencontres formelles

WHAT TO EXPECT

How formal do you need to be? When meeting a French person for the first time, or when meeting French people in a formal context, you need to be a bit of a copycat. Take your cue from the French as to how formal you need to be. When in doubt, be formal and wait for the French person to give you permission to be less so.

If you are from a culture where an informal dress style or a relaxed interaction between people is acceptable, you will probably need to adapt when in France. French people will feel ill at ease if the codes they use are not being observed. If you address them by their first name when you barely know each other, they will not know how to respond; for them to use your first name straightaway would often be unthinkable. Forget to shake hands and you may be considered rude.

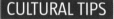
CULTURAL TIPS

In a formal context, instead of simply thanking someone by saying *"merci"*, you can be very polite and say:
— *Je vous remercie.*

When addressing or referring to people with a specific function or title, you generally use *Monsieur* and the profession or title as in *"Monsieur le juge"*, *"Monsieur le Président"*, *"Monsieur le Maire"*, *"Monsieur le Comte"*. Similarly, you would say *"Madame le Maire"*, *"Madame le juge"* and *"Madame la Marquise"*. Exceptions are lawyers and notaries, who are addressed as *Maître* for both men and women, and doctors, both male and female, who are addressed as *Docteur*.

TAKE YOUR CUE FROM THE FRENCH AS TO HOW FORMAL YOU NEED TO BE.

Les rencontres formelles

Talk too loudly in public or display a very friendly manner and you will be considered badly brought up. As for using the informal *tu* when addressing a French adult, you should definitely avoid it.

Even if the French, particularly younger people, are gradually becoming a little less formal, there are still many barriers between a formal and informal relationship. The French may be beginning to feel more at ease with using first names with people they meet frequently, in the workplace for example, but they won't expect to call their bank manager, accountant, doctor or even their neighbour by their first name. French society is very hierarchical and respect is shown to older people and people with a certain status.

Switching from using *vous* to *tu* remains very difficult, even when circumstances are appropriate. French people often explain that they have great difficulty using the *tu* form of the verb other than with family and very close friends. A younger person may find it particularly difficult to use *tu* to an older person, even if that person has requested that the young person do so. It is not uncommon to hear older people using *tu* with a daughter- or son-in-law, but as a sign of respect, the daughter- or son-in-law uses *vous*.

THE FRENCH ARE BEGINNING TO FEEL MORE AT EASE WITH USING FIRST NAMES WITH PEOPLE THEY MEET FREQUENTLY, IN THE WORKPLACE FOR EXAMPLE.

🔊 KEYWORDS

un médecin	doctor
un notaire	notary
un propriétaire	owner
un banquier	banker
le maire	mayor
une connaissance	an acquaintance
un cabinet	surgery/office
une étude	(notary's) office
un bureau	office
une poignée de main	handshake
une salutation	greeting
un rendez-vous	appointment
une prise de contact	first meeting
un agenda	diary/datebook
le vouvoiement	adressing somebody as *vous*
vouvoyer	to address somebody as *vous*
serrer la main à quelqu'un	to shake hands with somebody
consulter	to consult, seek advice from

Les rencontres formelles

CULTURAL TIPS

When invited to a formal occasion or a business meeting, men should always wear a tie and jacket and only remove their jacket if they are invited to do so.

Monsieur Tout-le-monde is the man in the street and *Monsieur Untel* is Mr So-and-so.

If you meet someone for a second time in the same day, you can jokingly say *"Rebonjour"*. You should always greet the person again, without shaking their hand, or at least smile and nod your head as you pass.

When talking about the wife of the person you are speaking to, you should refer to her as *votre épouse* or *votre dame* rather than *votre femme*. For a man, you use *votre époux*.

If you have a formal appointment or meeting with a French person, they will accompany you to the door when you have finished. They will indicate that they are intending to do this by saying:
– *Je vous accompagne.*

Some aspects of formality will be the same whether the French person is someone you know well or not. You should always greet people individually upon arriving and leaving. The form of the greeting and the accompanying gesture, a handshake in most cases, will depend on the nature of the relationship and how well you know the other person or persons, but you should never skip a greeting or make a general greeting to a group of people unless they are all strangers and in a public place.

As the gap between formality and informality is a delicate area for French people too, they will often resolve the problem by specifically requesting or granting permission to change to a less formal relationship. *"On peut peut-être se tutoyer ?"* (Shall we use *tu* with each other?) If a French person suggests this, it is an important sign of acceptance, but it may never happen, even if you are on a first-name basis. Surprisingly, French people sometimes move on to first names and giving a kiss, *une bise*, without it implying the use of *tu*. So, unless the French person requests a change, you should remain on a formal footing and adapt your manners and speech accordingly.

YOU SHOULD NEVER SKIP A GREETING OR MAKE A GENERAL GREETING TO A GROUP OF PEOPLE UNLESS THEY ARE ALL STRANGERS AND IN A PUBLIC PLACE.

 IDIOMS

– *Une rencontre au sommet* is a summit meeting.
– *Cela ne se rencontre plus de nos jours* means one doesn't come across that anymore.
– *Les grands esprits se rencontrent* means great minds think alike.
– *Le métro quand il fait chaud, bonjour les dégâts* means when it's hot in the metro system, it's absolute hell!

Les rencontres formelles

HISTORY AND TRADITIONS

Madame, as a form of address, was originally used when referring to ladies of noble birth, particularly to the daughters of the royal family. *Mademoiselle* was used for untitled ladies. From the 17th century on, *Madame* began to be used when referring to married women in the bourgeois classes, too, and *Mademoiselle* came to be used for unmarried women only. This distinction continued well into the 20th century, even when the terms came to be used when addressing women of all classes.

Monsieur followed a similar evolution, although this form of address was temporarily replaced during the Revolution by *Citoyen*. By the beginning of the 20th century, its usage was no longer reserved for men of the bourgeois classes, but for men in general.

 USEFUL PHRASES

– *Bonjour, Monsieur.*
Good morning/afternoon.
– *Bonjour, Madame, j'ai rendez-vous avec le docteur Martin.*
Good morning. I have an appointment with Dr Martin.
– *Enchanté de vous connaître.*
Nice to meet you.
– *Je suis heureux de faire votre connaissance.*
Pleased to meet you.
– *Bonjour, je suis le père de David.*
Hello, I'm David's father.
– *Au revoir, Monsieur.*
Goodbye.
– *Je suis très contente de vous avoir rencontré.*
I'm really pleased to have met you.
– *Passez une bonne journée !*
Have a good day!

Les rencontres formelles

CULTURAL TIPS

An invitation in writing will use even more formal language than that used when you actually meet someone, so do not be taken by surprise by the formality and complexity of the language. Similarly, when finishing a letter, the French will use an elaborate phrase that is simply the equivalent of sending their kind regards. When replying, you can simply use the same phrase and adapt it if there is a name included.

When you address someone as *Monsieur*, you should remember to add *Monsieur* at the end of the sentence when thanking or asking questions of the person. If it becomes too repetitive, you can omit this occasionally.

If you go to someone's house or office, upon entering you should wait for the other person to ask you to be seated. They will generally say:
– *Asseyez-vous, je vous en prie.*

Je vous en prie is a very useful little phrase. If somebody thanks you, you can use this phrase to acknowledge the person's thanks.

There is no equivalent of the Anglo-Saxon 'Ms' in French, but nowadays it is safer to use *Madame* for all women, married or not, unless you are referring to a young lady. *Mademoiselle* is no longer used on most official forms, but you will still hear *Mademoiselle* used when a young lady, such as a waitress, a shop assistant or a teenage girl is being addressed.

Tutoyer or *vouvoyer*, that is, the use of *tu* or *vous* when addressing family members, has also changed over the years. In certain families, particularly aristocratic ones, children were expected to use *vous* when addressing their parents. Sometimes husbands would use *tu* to their wives but expected their wives to use *vous* in return.

Using *tu* to a stranger, particularly in anger, is often meant as a form of insult. The police in France have been told to avoid using *tu* to young people when they question or arrest them.

🔊 YOU WILL HEAR

– *Bonjour, c'est Monsieur Perrotin, n'est-ce pas ?*
 Hello, it's Mr Perrotin, isn't it?
– *Madame Blanc, comment allez-vous ?*
 Mrs Blanc, how are you?
– *Ravi de vous rencontrer.*
 Pleased to meet you.
– *Bonjour à votre épouse.*
 Please say hello to your wife for me.
– *Ça m'a fait plaisir de vous revoir.*
 Delighted to have met you again.
– *Au revoir, à une prochaine fois.*
 Goodbye, see you again.
– *Bonne promenade !*
 Enjoy your walk!
– *Bonne fin d'après-midi !*
 Enjoy the rest of the afternoon!

Les rencontres formelles

🔊 LANGUAGE TIPS

When meeting people for the first time, you need to remember to observe the formalities. If you forget this, you may get off on the wrong foot. You will often find that you can follow the lead of the French person and copy their degree of formality and also their phrases. So if somebody says:
– *Je suis très content de vous rencontrer.*

you can simply reply:
– *Je suis très content de vous rencontrer aussi.*

Alternatively, when somebody says:
– *Enchanté !*

you can just respond:
– *Moi aussi.*

If they address you as *Madame* or *Monsieur*, you know you should definitely be addressing them in the same manner.

🔊 *Remember*

When entering a public area where there are already other people, for example, when you go into a shop, a waiting room or a bank, you should greet everybody by saying:
– *Bonjour Messieurs, Dames.*
Good morning, everyone.

Sometimes the word *bonjour* is omitted and you will hear French people simply say:
– *Messieurs, Dames.*

Un rendez-vous is an appointment, but the word can also be used figuratively:
– *Le soleil était au rendez-vous pour la fête.*
It was a sunny day for the party.

– *C'était un rendez-vous manqué.*
It was a wasted opportunity.

🔊 ADVANCED USEFUL PHRASES

– *Madame Trichet, ça fait plaisir de vous voir.*
Mrs Trichet, how nice to see you.
– *Bonjour Monsieur, ça fait un moment que je ne vous ai pas vu.*
Good morning, I haven't seen you for a while.
– *Saluez-le de ma part, s'il vous plaît.*
Please give him my regards.
– *Transmettez-lui mon meilleur souvenir.*
Give him my regards.
– *Ma mère vous envoie son bon souvenir.*
My mother sends you her greetings.
– *C'est votre petit-fils, je pense ?*
Is this your grandson, then?
– *Bien, je vais vous quitter.*
Well, I must be off.
– *Je vous laisse continuer votre chemin.*
I'll let you go on your way.

 **LEARN MORE**

For examples of greetings in informal situations, you can refer to *Les rencontres informelles*, p.45.

There are examples of using the *tu* form of the verb in *La famille*, p.52.

Les rencontres formelles

Most famous

The most commonly used greeting when meeting someone in France is *bonjour*. This word, introduced in the 13th century, had become a common greeting by the 15th and 16th centuries. It is still used no matter what the time of day. In French-speaking Canada, it is also used to mean goodbye.

French people will generally use the expression *au revoir* when saying goodbye. *Adieu*, an equivalent of "God be with you", was common usage from the 12th century onwards, but in the 17th century, the expression *au revoir* appeared and became interchangeable with *adieu*. It was only at the beginning of the 19th century that a distinction was made between the two, with *adieu* coming to mean a more definitive separation, such as death. Nowadays, the use of the word *adieu* is more common in expressions such as *faire ses adieux*, meaning to say one's farewells.

Quiz

Fill in the blanks using the verbs below.   A

passer, envoyer, saluer, faire, accompagner, rencontrer

D   F   E   C   B

A. *Je suis ravi de vous _____.*

B. *Je vous _____ à la porte.*

C. *Je suis heureux de _____ votre connaissance.*

D. *_____ une bonne journée.*

E. *_____-la de ma part, s'il vous plaît.*

F. *Ma sœur vous _____ son bon souvenir.*

Answers: A. *rencontrer*, B. *accompagne*, C. *faire*, D. *passez*, E. *saluez*, F. *envoie*.

KEY POINTS

Les rencontres formelles...

- require you to use *Madame* or *Monsieur* when addressing people.
- are accompanied by formal greetings.
- imply the use of the *vous* form of the verb.
- require correct dress.
- can involve signs of deference.

Les rencontres informelles

Les rencontres informelles

WHAT TO EXPECT

Watch French people greet each other and you will be able to see immediately how well they know each other. If they shake hands, then you are observing people who don't know each other well or who have a formal relationship. If they kiss each other on both cheeks, then you are watching people who are either related or who are friends. When several people meet, there will sometimes be a mixture of the two, as some people will know each other well and others less so.

Kissing on the cheek, *faire la bise* as the French call it, is often a bit of a mystery to people who are not used to the custom. How many kisses? Which side do you start with? Do you really kiss the cheek? The big question is, of course, whom, if anybody, do you kiss?

The French seem to *faire la bise* very easily and naturally. For others it can be awkward or clumsy. As always when it is a question of manners, you should let the French person indicate that they are expecting to *faire une bise*. They may well announce it by saying, *"On se fait la bise ?"* This can occur at the end of a dinner or after a shared experience or celebration. Generally you will already be on a first-name basis or will simultaneously start using first names. A French person suggesting you move to this form of greeting is not proposing, however, that you can start using the *tu* form of the verb. That would suggest an even greater degree of friendship.

CULTURAL TIPS

Young people are far less formal than older French people and it is common practice for teenagers and students to greet each other with a *bise* even on a first meeting. Usually, though, this will not be the case between boys, who will greet each other with a handshake unless they are very good friends already. Younger children will greet each other, too, and it is common as children gather for school to see boys shaking hands and girls giving a *bise* to both female and male friends.

If you want to acknowledge someone's thanks in an informal situation when you use *tu* with the person, you can simply say, *"Je t'en prie."*

Les rencontres informelles

The number of *bises* varies from two, one on each cheek, to four on alternating cheeks. Whether it's two, three or four depends on the region and family habits. As a rule of thumb, the further south you are, the more likely it is to be three or four kisses. It is best to presume it is two but be ready to continue! It will never be only one. Generally, you will start with the left cheek of the person opposite you, but again this is not a hard and fast rule. If you wear glasses and the other person does too, it is polite to remove them first.

CULTURAL TIPS

When moving to an informal relationship with a French person, it is not only the obvious signs that change, such as the use of first names or the manner of greeting, but also there will be a general relaxation in the language used. There will be more use of slang and less formal turns of phrase. Should you begin to use *tu* with a French friend, this will be even more noticeable.

One of the indications of less formal language will be the way people refer to each other. A girl's boyfriend will be referred to as her *jules*, a girl will become *une nana* and a man *un mec*. These terms are not necessarily pejorative, but they can be, so it is best to avoid using them yourself.

SINCE THE FRENCH TEND TO STAY IN THE REGION WHERE THEY WERE BROUGHT UP, FRIENDSHIPS ARE OFTEN LONG-TERM.

 IDIOMS

- *Faire ami-ami avec quelqu'un* is to be buddy-buddy with someone.
- *Le meilleur ami de l'homme* is man's best friend.
- *Je vous fais un prix d'ami* means 'I'll let you have it at a reduced price'.
- *Ils sont copains comme cochons* means they are as thick as thieves.
- *Poser un lapin à quelqu'un* is not to turn up for a meeting or to stand someone up.

Les rencontres informelles

When you exchange *bises*, you may not actually touch the other person. Often it is just a kissing sound near the other person's cheek. Usually, though, you will at least touch cheeks, but a *bise* is rarely a big kiss firmly planted on somebody's cheek unless it is between members of the same family. Some people will accompany a *bise* by placing a hand lightly on the upper arm of the other person but others will just lean forward without touching.

For French people, it is essential to greet each person individually upon arriving and departing in a manner that is appropriate to the nature of the relationship. So if you exchanged *bises* as you met, you will need to repeat the action as you leave!

🔊 KEYWORDS

un ami/une amie	friend
un copain/une copine	friend, mate/buddy
un pote	mate/buddy
une bise	kiss
un bisou	kiss, peck
Salut !	Hello! Hi!
Ça va ?	How are things?
Ça roule ?	How's life?
Ciao !	Bye!
À plus !	See you later!
Bon courage !	Good luck! All the best!
Je t'appelle.	I'll call you.
chez moi	my place, my house
boire un coup	to have a drink
manger un bout	to have a bite to eat
tutoyer	to address somebody as *tu*
saluer	to greet
faire la bise	to give somebody a kiss
faire un bisou	to give somebody a kiss

Les rencontres informelles

CULTURAL TIPS

In informal French, words are often shortened. So *l'après-midi*, the afternoon, becomes *l'aprèm*. Similarly, *les actualités*, the news, becomes *les actus*, *la boulangerie* is shortened to *la boulange* and *un ordinateur*, a computer, is referred to as *un ordi*. Some words change almost completely so *le cinéma* becomes *le cinoche*, *facile*, meaning easy, becomes *fastoche* and *un rendez-vous* becomes *un rencard*. You do not need to use these words yourself, but it is useful to be able to recognise them and fun to spot them.

When leaving somebody, you can tell him you'll see him soon by saying *"À plus"*. When texting or emailing, French people will write this as A+.

🔊 USEFUL PHRASES

– *Bonjour, tu vas bien ?*
   Hello, how are you?
– *Salut ! Comment ça va ?*
   Hi! How are things?
– *Je ne t'ai pas vu depuis un moment.*
   I haven't seen you for a while.
– *En forme ?*
   Fighting fit / Doing okay?
– *Tout va bien ?*
   Everything going well?
– *Et ta copine. Comment va-t-elle ?*
   How's your girlfriend doing?
– *Bon, je te laisse.*
   Okay, I'll be off.
– *Bien, il faut que je file.*
   Okay, I must dash.
– *Salut ! À plus.*
   Bye. See you soon.
– *À un de ces jours.*
   See you around.

HISTORY AND TRADITIONS

The most common greeting in informal relationships is *"Salut !"* meaning "Hi!" The word originally had a religious connotation from its link to *sauver*, meaning to save. However, as early as the 11th century, it became a form of civility when meeting and leaving people. Its use as an exclamation was associated with wishing someone health and prosperity. In the 17th century, it was already being used simply as a brief word of welcome or goodbye without a religious connotation. Today, it is a familiar version of *bonjour* and *au revoir*.

As an informal greeting, it is also possible to say *"Coucou"*. This is particularly used when saying hello to a baby, but is also used as a greeting on an impromptu visit or when trying to find out if anybody is there when entering a house.

Recently *bye*, borrowed from English, has also come to be used informally as an alternative to *au revoir*.

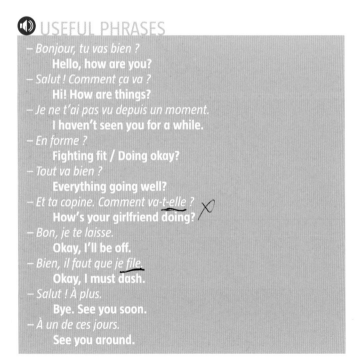

Les rencontres informelles

🔊 Remember

When someone talks about a friend in French, it is not always possible to tell whether a man or a woman is being talked about. As the masculine possessive *mon* is used because of the initial vowel in *ami*, you cannot hear a difference. Only in writing, if there is an 'e' at the end of *amie*, do you know that the friend is female. This can lead to some intriguing situations!

Une copine is used by women when talking about a female friend. When used by a man it can mean his special girlfriend, and then he will refer to her as *ma copine*, but depending on the context he may also just be referring to a friend who is female.

A mate or buddy is *un pote*.

🔊 YOU WILL HEAR

– *Bien. Et toi ?*
   Fine/good, and you?
– *Impec !*
   Great!
– *Ça roule.*
   I'm doing fine/well.
– *On fait comme ça.*
   Let's do that, then.
– *Tiens-moi au courant.*
   Let me know how it goes.
– *Tu me passes un coup de fil ?*
   Will you give me a call?
– *Tu m'envoies un texto ?*
   Will you send me a text message?
– *Tu me diras pour mardi ?*
   Will you let me know for Tuesday?

🔊 ADVANCED USEFUL PHRASES

– *Tiens ! Comment vas-tu ?*
   Hello! How are you?
– *Salut ! Ça fait plaisir de te voir.*
   Hi! Good to see you.
– *Je te fais la bise.*
   Let me give you a kiss.
– *Ça fait un moment qu'on ne s'est pas vu.*
   We haven't seen each other for ages.
– *Ça te dit d'aller boire un coup ?*
   Do you fancy/How about going for a drink?
– *J'aimerais que tu rencontres ma copine.*
   I'd like you to meet my girlfriend.
– *Il faut que je coure, je suis en retard.*
   I'll have to run, I'm late.
– *Je te dis au revoir.*
   Goodbye, then.

Les rencontres informelles

LANGUAGE TIPS

When in an informal situation with people using first names and saying *tu* to each other, and when you are sure you are expected to use *tu* also, try to use it consistently. If you are not used to using this form of the verb it is easy to forget and mix in some sentences where you use the *vous* form. Remember also to be consistent and use first names with *tu*. You should not use *tu* and then address the same person as *Monsieur*.

Sometimes in a mixed group there will be people with whom you can use *tu* and others with whom you need to use *vous*, so you need to be on your guard and try to remember which form of the verb you should be using. It's not always easy and occasionally even French people will slip up.

CULTURAL TIPS

Remember to use *tu* when addressing young children. You can start saying *vous* to young people you don't know around the age of 16 or 17.

Frequently nowadays French people use the Italian word 'ciao' when saying goodbye. This is particularly true at the end of a phone call.

If an animal is pestering you and you want it to go away, you will of course use the *tu* form of the verb and say, *"Va-t-en!"*

Sometimes members of the same club or association, or people practising a sport together, will start using *tu* almost immediately. In these cases it is a sign of unity and of belonging to a group with a shared interest.

Since the French tend to stay in the region where they were brought up, friendships are often long-term. This has the effect of leaving little space for newer close friendships and tends to increase the barriers between formal and less-formal relationships.

 **LEARN MORE**

For examples of using the *tu* form of the verb, you can refer to *La famille*, p.52.

For formal expressions of greeting, you can refer to *Les rencontres formelles*, p.38.

Les rencontres informelles

Most famous

The much-loved French singer Georges Brassens wrote a song titled 'Les Copains d'Abord' (1964). The song, which was written as the theme song for a film called LES COPAINS, is a tribute to friendship. It is known by all generations and is one of Brassen's most popular songs. It is instantly recognisable because of the catchy repetition of the song's title. Literally the title means 'Mates come first', but in French there is a play on words as it also sounds like *les copains de bord*, meaning 'shipmates first and foremost'. The song relates friendship to the strong ties of shipmates.

The word *copain*, meaning friend, came originally from the old French word *compain*, meaning companion. This 15th century spelling had changed to the modern word *copain* by the 20th century. Today, the word means a good friend and there is a strong element of affection implied.

Quiz

Match the first half of the sentence with its second half.

4 **A.** *Salut ! Comment...* **1.** *un coup de fil.*
5 **B.** *On se fait...* **2.** *je file.* \ dash
6 **C.** *Je veux te présenter...* **3.** *nana sympathique.*
2 **D.** *Il faut que...* **4.** *vas-tu ?*
1 **E.** *Tu me passes...* **5.** *la bise ?*
3 **F.** *Alice est une...* **6.** *ma copine.*

Answers: A4, B5, C6, D2, E1, F3.

Les rencontres informelles...

- imply using first names.
- do not automatically allow you to use the *tu* form of the verb.
- may mean you greet people with a *bise*.
- involve less formal language.
- are accompanied by greetings such as *Salut !*

La famille

WHAT TO EXPECT

Several children are eating their salad starter with obvious enjoyment. *Grand-mère*, seated at one end of the table, and *Grand-père*, seated at the other end, look on proudly while *Maman* and *Papa*, seated in the middle, are having a lively political discussion. A typical French family is enjoying a long Sunday lunch.

In France, *la famille* plays a very central role in everyday life. Latin cultures traditionally place a lot of emphasis on the family, and in France, families with six or seven children were common in the 1950s and 1960s. Although most French couples now have fewer children, the concept of the large, extended family remains as many French people have experienced it personally.

ALTHOUGH MOST FRENCH COUPLES NOW HAVE FEWER CHILDREN, THE CONCEPT OF THE LARGE, EXTENDED FAMILY REMAINS.

CULTURAL TIPS

As a foreigner you may find that French people will use your first name more easily than they would the first name of a French person. This is because your surname may be difficult for them to pronounce and they will find it easier to introduce you by your first name.

If you are staying with a French family, you will see that the family members greet each other with *bises*, kisses on the cheek, every morning and similarly before going to bed. The number of *bises* will depend on the family tradition and the region. The persons who have married into the family will have adapted, even if in their own family the number of *bises* given was different.

La famille

In addition to their families, the French are also very attached to their home region, and consequently there is less geographical mobility than in Anglo-Saxon countries, for example. Many French people experience what they feel is a sort of exile if, for their studies or work, they have to move away from their home, even when the distance is only a short one. Generally, members of the same family tend to live relatively near to each other and remain in close, often daily, contact. This can result in little free time for other social relationships and explains why people arriving in a new area can experience difficulty in establishing new contacts. Family life simply doesn't leave much time for a large social circle of friends.

◀) KEYWORDS

la belle-mère	mother-in-law
le beau-père	father-in-law
la belle-famille	in-laws
le gendre	son-in-law
la tante	aunt
l'oncle	uncle
le neveu	nephew
la nièce	niece
le cousin germain	first cousin
la grand-mère	grandmother
le grand-père	grandfather
les petits-enfants	grandchildren
les arrière-petits-enfants	great-grandchildren
l'aîné des garçons	the eldest boy
la cadette des filles	the youngest daughter
un enfant unique	only child
un anniversaire	birthday, anniversary
faire une fête	to have a party

◀) IDIOMS

- *Laver son linge sale en famille* is to wash one's dirty linen in public/to air dirty laundry.
- *Il y a un air de famille* means there's a family likeness.
- If a man is referred to as *très famille* it means he is a real family man.
- *Le soutien de famille* is the breadwinner.

La famille

French families don't, of course, always get along well together, but there will be a shared belief in family duty and what is owed to the family. There will be frequent family gatherings as well as end-of-year holidays, birthdays and wedding anniversaries.

CULTURAL TIPS

When someone marries into a French family, the family members will usually use the informal *tu* when addressing the new arrival. They may have being doing so already. This does not mean that the new arrival will necessarily be able to use *tu* in return. Often the use of *tu* will be mutually adopted between people of the same generation while *vous* is maintained when addressing older members of the family, although this is less common than in the past. The French have no difficulty with relationships where some people use the informal *tu*, parents addressing a daughter-in-law, for example, while she responds using the formal *vous*.

The use of first names when addressing in-laws is now common. The most popular terms for grandparents are *Mamie* and *Papy*.

Some terms showing the relationship between two family members have two possible meanings. *La belle-mère* means mother-in-law, but also stepmother. Similarly *la belle-fille* means daughter-in-law, but also stepdaughter. Therefore, when you hear these terms, you need to be aware of the two possible interpretations.

The French believe it is unlucky to seat 13 people at a table, so sometimes at a family gathering there will be an extra place set to avoid having the unlucky 13 place settings.

Many French people also spend their vacations in the family's *maison de campagne*, the country home. This will either be the family home, probably originally belonging to the grandparents or great-grandparents, or a home in the country purchased specially for the family to be able to visit as a group. Family photos will be taken and displayed proudly afterwards to colleagues and friends.

Ironically, this tradition of families with several children is sometimes a consequence of higher divorce rates. New family groupings with children from previous marriages on both sides of the couple are more and more common. The French call these families *les familles recomposées*. Even though the number of civil contracts between couples and the number of divorces and children born out of wedlock continue to increase, in France the concept of *la famille* remains strong.

La famille

HISTORY AND TRADITIONS

Policies to encourage and protect large families, particularly poorer ones, have existed in France since the 19th century. After the Second World War, General de Gaulle, anxious to rebuild the population, introduced policies to encourage families to have several children. These policies were continued up to and through the 1970s, and there are still many subsidies and advantages for families with three or more children, known as *les familles nombreuses*.

The most well-known advantage is the *carte famille nombreuse*, which was established by the SNCF, the French railways, as early as 1921. It entitled these families to reductions in ticket prices and is still in existence.

THE MOST POPULAR TERMS
FOR GRANDPARENTS
ARE *MAMIE* AND *PAPY*.

USEFUL PHRASES

– *Je vous présente mon mari.*
    I'd like to introduce you to my husband.
– *C'est votre petite-fille ?*
    Is this your granddaughter?
– *Vous avez combien d'enfants ?*
    How many children do you have?
– *Je connais votre papa.*
    I know your father.
– *Vincent m'a parlé de vous.*
    Vincent has told me about you.
– *Bon anniversaire !*
    Happy birthday!
– *Tu connais ma fille ?*
    Do you know my daughter?
– *Tu as quel âge ?*
    How old are you?

La famille

CULTURAL TIPS

When referring to the individuals who have become members of a family by marriage, for example, a daughter-in-law or a brother-in-law, a French family will sometimes jokingly refer to them as *les pièces rapportées*, a term used in sewing to mean patches, or added pieces.

Some terms for family relationships have slang versions. The most frequently used terms are *la belle-doche* for *la belle-mère*, which is pejorative, and *le beauf* for *le beau-frère*, which is affectionate. However, to say someone is *beauf* when you are not talking about a family relationship is to say that the person is narrow-minded and vulgar. *"Il est beauf"* is therefore not a flattering description.

When younger members of the family say they want to *"présenter quelqu'un"*, they do not mean simply introduce someone. Usually this is a special girlfriend or boyfriend and the introduction to the family shows it is a serious relationship.

Allowances to help families reconcile their family and professional life also exist. There are allowances and tax reductions to help mothers pay for help to look after their children while they work, family allowances for families with two or more children and fixed amounts for children of poorer families to help cover the costs of school supplies at the beginning of each academic year.

Today the French have the highest fertility rate in Europe with an average of more than two children per woman.

🔊 YOU WILL HEAR

— *Venez rencontrer tout le monde.*
   Come and meet everyone.
— *Je ne crois pas que vous connaissez mon frère.*
   I don't think you know my brother.
— *Voici mes deux enfants.*
   Here are my two children.
— *Votre aîné a quel âge ?*
   How old is your eldest?
— *Votre mari est très sympathique.*
   Your husband is really nice.
— *On fait un petit repas de famille dimanche.*
   We're having a family meal on Sunday.
— *Je fais une petite fête pour ma fille samedi. Pouvez-vous venir ?*
   I'm having a little party for my daughter on Saturday. Can you come?
— *Nous allons fêter les cinquante ans de mariage de mes parents ce week-end.*
   We're celebrating my parents' 50th wedding anniversary this weekend.

La famille

 LANGUAGE TIPS

When addressing the different members of a French family, you will need to remember to use the informal *tu* with some members and not with others. There will probably be several generations of a family present for a meal or special celebration and it is very unlikely that the older generations will expect you to use *tu*, although you will use *tu* when addressing any young children present. Don't be surprised if very young children say *tu* to you; they usually only become aware of the need to use the formal *vous* to some people around the age of seven.

For speaking to young children, it's useful to have some stock phrases prepared such as:
– *Comment t'appelles-tu ?*
– *Quel âge as-tu ?*
– *Tu aimes l'école ?*

 *Remember*

When you are with a French family, you will hear various terms of endearment used between the family members. Between adults, the most common terms are *chérie* or *ma chérie*, meaning darling. For children there are a vast number of terms, some of which may appear surprising. Addressing a child as my flea (*ma puce*), my cabbage (*mon chou*) or my rabbit (*mon lapin)* may seem odd, but the French commonly use such terms when young children are concerned. You will not need to use them, but it is fun to become familiar with them.

 ADVANCED USEFUL PHRASES

– *J'ai beaucoup entendu parler de vous.*
 I've heard a lot about you.
– *Je suis ravi de vous rencontrer enfin.*
 I'm really pleased to finally meet you.
– *Votre famille est originaire de quelle région ?*
 Which region does your family come from?
– *Vous avez une très grande famille.*
 You've got a really big family.
– *Est-ce que vous avez des arrière-petits-enfants ?*
 Do you have any great-grandchildren?
– *Vous avez une très belle maison de famille.*
 You have a lovely family home.
– *J'ai apporté un petit cadeau pour Amandine.*
 I've brought a small present for Amandine.
– *La fête était très sympa.*
 It was a really nice party.

 **LEARN MORE**

For other examples of using the *tu* form of the verb, you can refer to *Les rencontres informelles*, p.45.

You can find more information on family celebrations in *Un mariage*, p.29.

La famille

Most famous

As France is a republic, there is no official royal family. However, there are descendants of two branches of the royal family, the House of Bourbon and the House of Orléans. French royalists are divided as to which family is the most legitimate.

The House of Bourbon can be traced back to Henri IV. The current head of the House of Bourbon is Louis de Bourbon who was born in 1974 and has French nationality through his grandmother. In the royalist press he is known as Louis XX and he is a descendant of Philippe V of Spain, who was the *duc d'Anjou* before his succession to the Spanish throne.

The House of Orléans, a cadet branch of the House of Bourbon, also goes back to Henri IV. The *comte de Paris et duc de France*, born in 1933 and known as Henri VII by his supporters, is the current head of this branch. The family was exiled by law for many years in England, Morocco and then Belgium until the law was abolished in 1950. Prince Henri moved to Paris and today travels around France pursuing the aims of his association, the *Institut de la Maison Royale de France*.

Quiz

Read the information about the Martin family and then answer the questions below.

Marie est la femme de Georges. Valérie est la maman d'Yves. Thomas est le petit-fils de Robert. Jacques est le beau-frère de Robert. Robert est le beau-père d'Alice. Marie est la belle-mère de Robert. Anne est l'arrière petite-fille de Marie. Valérie est la fille de Georges. Georges est le père de Jacques.

A. *Qui est le frère d'Anne ?* ___Thomas___
B. *Qui est le beau-fils de Georges ?* ___Robert___
C. *Qui est la fille d'Yves ?* ___Anne___
D. *Qui est le frère de Valérie ?* ___Jacques___
E. *Qui est la mère de Thomas ?* ___Alice___
✓ **F.** *Qui est le fils de Marie ?* ___Jacques___

Answers: A. Thomas, B. Robert, C. Anne, D. Jacques, E. Alice, F. Jacques.

KEY POINTS

La famille...

- is extremely important in France.
- often has many members.
- meets frequently for social occasions.
- often stays close to its roots.
- dominates the time for social relationships.

Les différences régionales

Les différences régionales

WHAT TO EXPECT

How different is a French person from Marseille versus one from Bordeaux, Quimper or Paris? The French themselves certainly believe there are differences and strongly defend their various regional identities. Asserting these regional identities can take the form of political actions as in the Basque region and Corsica, or cultural expression as in Brittany, where the Breton language is kept alive with special schools and festivals. It is also seen throughout France in the humorous portrayal of regional stereotypes in films and comic strips.

The sense of place, as exemplified by the concept of *terroir*, the identity that the soil confers on the products of a particular region, is deeply rooted in a country with a strong attachment to the land and rural life. Even if more French people now live in cities than in rural areas, the attachment to the countryside remains strong. It is reflected in the variety and quality of regional cooking and products and the concept of *La France profonde*, rural France. The French in general are very proud of their home region, even if they live in Paris.

CULTURAL TIPS

French as it is spoken in the city of Tours and the surrounding region is recognised as being the best French accent.

In the South of France, people use the informal *tu* form of the verb more easily than in the North. In general, the language register is more relaxed in the South, but this does depend on the context and you should not presume that you can use *tu* when addressing French people unless they ask you to, even in the South.

People in the East of France are considered to be more punctual than people in the South. The inhabitants of Lyon, the gateway to the South, refer to the *petit quart d'heure lyonnais* when they are speaking about concerts or events that usually start about 15 minutes after the announced time, for example.

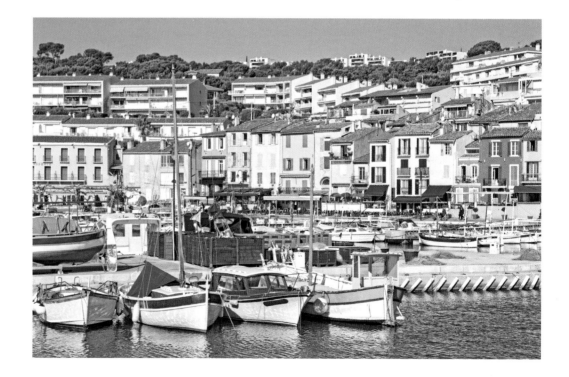

Les différences régionales

There are two major divisions in France. The first is that between Paris and the provinces. Both culturally and educationally, the French Republic has attempted to maintain a high degree of uniformity, the most obvious example being French school programmes. These are the same throughout France and are decided in Paris. It is often said, however, that Paris is not France, and in the provinces it can seem as if there is a different reality that is not always recognised, although politicians nowadays do make more of an effort to visit the regions to show they are in touch with the country as a whole.

The second major division is between the North and the South of the country. Even the weather observes this break in continuity. Listen to weather bulletins in France and you will frequently hear the forecast given for the weather North of the Loire River and South of the Loire. This river is seen to cut France in half horizontally, although most French people would situate the real South as starting somewhat below the Loire.

THE FRENCH STRONGLY DEFEND THEIR VARIOUS REGIONAL IDENTITIES.

CULTURAL TIPS

It is often said that you can hear the sun in the Provencal accent. This accent has a nasal twang and all the syllables in words are sounded out, including the normally silent final 'e's. *Vin*, wine, becomes *veng*, and France becomes *France-uh*.

People from Marseille are said to exaggerate a lot. The most often cited example is the sardine that blocked the entrance to the port! This story is based on a historical event when a boat called the *Sartine*, spelled with a 't', was sunk by the British in 1780, thus blocking, for a time, access to the port. The name was transformed to 'sardine' with a 'd' as people spoke about the event, and from then on the story was used to refer to the people of Marseille's tendency to exaggerate.

 IDIOMS

— *Faire une réponse de Normand* means to neither say yes nor no.
— *Une promesse de Gascon* is an empty or vain promise.
— *Une histoire marseillaise* is a tall story.
— *Faire du Paris* is to focus excessively on Paris.

Les différences régionales

Ask why something isn't working in the South of France and you will often be answered with a Gallic shrug and the apparently self-explanatory comment, *"C'est le Sud."* Ask somebody from the South to envisage life in the North of France and the reaction will very often be one of horror, as was so humorously portrayed in a recent, enormously successful film about the transfer of a post office worker from the South to the North.

When visiting France, you will also experience these regional differences in the various French accents you will hear. Relating the word for bread, *pain*, as pronounced in Paris to the *peng* you will hear in Provence, is not always obvious. You will discover and delight in regional diversity in both the French lifestyle and the French language.

WHEN VISITING FRANCE, YOU WILL ALSO EXPERIENCE REGIONAL DIFFERENCES IN THE VARIOUS FRENCH ACCENTS YOU WILL HEAR.

🔊 KEYWORDS

un accent	accent
un patois	dialect
l'argot	slang
bretonnant	Breton-speaking
un Parisien	a Parisian
la capitale	capital
les provinces	provinces
le Sud	the South of France
le Nord	the North of France
l'Est	the East of France
l'Ouest	the West of France
une région	region
un costume traditionnel	traditional costume
la musique traditionnelle	traditional music
la danse folklorique	country dancing
la cuisine régionale	regional cooking
parler	to speak
jurer	to swear

Les différences régionales

CULTURAL TIPS

People in the North of France think of themselves as more *sérieux*, that is more reliable, than people in the South of France.

The number of *bises*, or kisses, given as greetings in the South is usually three or four on alternate cheeks. In the North, it is generally two.

In the North of France around Lille, the inhabitants are called Ch'tis. The original *patois*, or dialect, is no longer spoken very much, but certain *patois* expressions are used frequently in the region. The accent has a characteristic and predominant 'ch' sound so that *ça va* is pronounced as *cha va*. Vowels are also pronounced differently so that *pas* becomes *pos*.

Most regions of France have traditional dances and music and sometimes even traditional instruments. The Brittany region is probably the most famous example of this with its festivals of Celtic music and the *biniou*, a sort of bagpipe with only one drone.

THE INHABITANTS OF LYON REFER TO THE *PETIT QUART D'HEURE LYONNAIS* WHEN THEY ARE SPEAKING ABOUT CONCERTS OR EVENTS THAT USUALLY START ABOUT 15 MINUTES AFTER THE ANNOUNCED TIME.

USEFUL PHRASES

— *Vous êtes Parisien ?*
Are you from Paris?
— *Vous aimez Paris ?*
Do you like Paris?
— *Vous êtes de quelle région ?*
Which region are you from?
— *Votre famille est du Sud, je crois ?*
Your family is from the South of France, isn't it?
— *Vous parlez breton ?*
Do you speak Breton?
— *Je ne connais pas cette tradition.*
I'm not familiar with this tradition.
— *C'est spécifique à cette région ?*
Is it specific to this region?
— *Qu'est-ce que je dois faire ?*
What am I supposed to do?

Les différences régionales

HISTORY AND TRADITIONS

From a linguistic point of view, France used to be divided into two parts. A northern part, where the *langue d'Oïl* was spoken, and a southern part, where people used the *langue d'Oc*, or Occitan. Exceptions to this were the Basque region and Brittany.

Occitan dates from the 10th century, but its use declined from the 14th century onwards, and in 1539 it was decreed that the *langue d'Oïl* was to be used for all French administrative purposes. Occitan remained, however, the everyday language for people living in the rural areas of the South of France until the early 20th century.

Gradually, as French was enforced in all regions by the central government in Paris, local *patois* or dialects began to die out. From 1882, schools were required to teach in French and children were punished for using *patois*. This belief in imposing unity and uniformity meant that, until very recently, having a strong regional accent was a disadvantage when seeking employment.

🔊 YOU WILL HEAR

– *Vous connaissez cette région ?*
   Do you know this region?
– *Vous comprenez l'accent provençal ?*
   Do you understand the Provençal accent?
– *Qu'est-ce que vous pensez de la Provence ?*
   What do you think of Provence?
– *On va vous faire goûter la cuisine du Sud-Ouest.*
   We'll let you taste the cuisine of the Southwest of France.
– *Ici, on fait comme ça.*
   That's how we do it here.
– *C'est notre musique traditionnelle.*
   It's our traditional music.
– *Nous sommes fiers de notre région.*
   We are proud of our region.
– *Nous aimons notre village.*
   We love our village.

🔊 *Remember*

The further South you travel in France, the more likely you are to hear people using a lot of swear words. Many French swear words are not as strong as their equivalent in other languages and therefore not necessarily as shocking.

One of the most common swear words in French is *merde,* and this can be used in various forms: as an exclamation, as a verb (*merder*), as a noun (*la merde*), or as an adjective (*merdeux* and *merdique*). The tone of voice usually indicates the intention of the speaker and this can vary, for the same word, from teasing to insulting. There are also many linked words such as *emmerder quelqu'un* (to get on someone's nerves), or *un emmerdeur* (someone who is a pain in the neck), or *emmmerdant* (annoying), or *un emmerdement* (a hassle). Similarly *se démerder* also exists, meaning to manage or to get out of a mess.

It is always advisable to avoid using these words in French yourself, as it is easy to misjudge the appropriateness of their use.

Les différences régionales

When you are asking for things in shops, particularly when food is concerned, there may be local names that you don't know. Sometimes even words that you do know may be pronounced with an accent that makes it difficult for you to recognise them. In these cases, you can avoid problems by indicating or describing the item you wish to buy.

If you can see the article displayed, you can say:
– *Je voudrais le pain qui est en haut à gauche.*
I'd like the loaf at the top on the left.

– *Je voudrais le fromage qui est juste devant, s'il vous plaît.*
I'd like the cheese just in front, please.

– *J'aimerais le sandwich avec les tomates et du jambon, s'il vous plaît.*
I'd like the tomato and ham sandwich, please.

Most famous

The 2008 film Bienvenue chez les Ch'tis was based on the theme of regional differences and prejudices, in this case the fear of someone from the South of France transferred to a position in a small town in the North. As the character heads northwards, his reluctance reflected by the excessively slow speed he adopts on the motorway, a *gendarme*, a local policeman, stops him. When he explains his plight, the *gendarme* immediately commiserates and signals for him to continue without fining him. The horror of going to live in the North is immediately understood. The theme of unjustified prejudice is treated with great humour and the film was one of the highest-grossing French films ever.

The comic strip books built around the character Astérix, created by René Goscinny, also draw on regional as well as national stereotypes. Corsicans are portrayed as being lazy, Bretons as being insular and so on. The stereotypes are all part of a humorous parody of life in a historical Gaul that is not so different from France today.

 **LEARN MORE**

You can find further examples of asking for more information in *Un mariage*, p.29.

For examples of less formal language, you can refer to *Les rencontres informelles*, p.45.

Les différences régionales

MOST REGIONS OF FRANCE
HAVE TRADITIONAL DANCES
AND MUSIC.

🔊 ADVANCED USEFUL PHRASES

– Vous pouvez parler plus lentement, s'il vous plaît?
Can you speak more slowly, please?
– Je n'ai pas l'habitude de l'accent du Nord.
I'm not used to the accent in the North of France.
– J'ai un peu de mal avec l'accent de Marseille.
I find the Marseille accent a bit difficult.
– C'est un mot utilisé seulement dans cette région ?
Is it a word used only in this region?
– Vous pouvez m'expliquer le sens de ce mot, s'il vous plaît ?
Can you explain the meaning of this word, please?
– Quelles sont les caractéristiques de cette région ?
What are the characteristics of this region?
– Est-ce que cette musique est typique de cette région ?
Is this music typical of the region?
– Combien de bises fait-on par ici ?
How many kisses do people give around here?

Are the following statements true or false?

A. The inhabitants of Marseille are known for exaggeration.
❑ True ❑ False

B. The Ch'tis are from Brittany.
❑ True ❑ False

C. People in the east of France are known for never being on time.
❑ True ❑ False

D. The *langue d'Oc* was spoken in the southern part of France.
❑ True ❑ False

E. There is less prejudice against regional accents than in the past.
❑ True ❑ False

F. In the South of France, manners are often less formal than in the North.
❑ True ❑ False

Answers: A. True, B. False, C. False, D. True, E. True, F. True.

KEY POINTS

Les différences régionales...

- can be found in local dishes, traditional music and dance and regional products.
- are frequently echoed by a regional accent.
- often have a historical basis.
- are noticeable when comparing lifestyles between Paris and the provinces.
- are seen in the contrast between the North and the South of France.

As they say in French

- « *Les amis de nos amis sont nos amis.* »
  Proverbe français

- « *Les bons comptes font les bons amis.* »
  Proverbe français

  Good accounts make good friends

- « *Qu'un ami véritable est une douce chose !* »
  Jean de La Fontaine

  That a real friend is a sweet thing

- « *Dans toute mère de famille, il y une belle-mère qui sommeille.* »
  Francis de Croisset

- « *Avoir sa belle-mère en province quand on demeure à Paris, et vice versa, est une de ces bonnes fortunes qui se rencontrent toujours trop rarement.* »
  Honoré de Balzac

Part 3

WHAT TO SAY

La météo et la santé

WHAT TO EXPECT

If you're invited for an *apéritif*, or simply standing in a queue and want to practise your French, how do you start a conversation? When a French acquaintance greets you in the street, or when a French friend telephones you, what can you say to keep the conversation going? If a French person starts chatting to you, how do you respond?

Two common and easy topics are the weather, as in many countries, and people's health. The French are very talkative on both subjects and you will find that, if you have a few key words and phrases, you can carry on a conversation quite easily.

CULTURAL TIPS

Most French people usually head south for their vacation in July or August. In many cases, this destination is preferred because of the weather. It is well-known that after a poor summer in the north one year, there are more reservations in the south the following year. The periods of heavy two-way traffic during the summer weekends, when those departing cross with those arriving, are called *les chassés croisés*. The term is also heard in the winter as people travel to and from ski resorts.

the cross chales

Interestingly, in France, 'April showers' occur in March and are called *les giboulées de mars*.

Weather bulletins on television end by giving the time of sunrise and sunset for the next day and the resulting number of minutes of more or less sun.

IF YOU HAVE A FEW KEY WORDS AND PHRASES FOR THE WEATHER, YOU CAN CARRY ON A CONVERSATION QUITE EASILY.

La météo et la santé

The weather is an important topic for the French, but not just because most people usually prefers good weather to rain and cold. France remains a country where agriculture is very important and French people are very concerned if the weather isn't as it should be for a given time of year. Too much or too little rain affects crops, late frosts affect the many fruit-growing areas and, in particular, the wrong combination of rain and sun – or worse still, hailstorms – has an effect on the grape harvest and the quality of that year's wine. Most French people are therefore very attuned to these problems and there are many references to the weather in newspapers, on television and, of course, in everyday conversations.

Another aspect of the weather that is of great importance to the French is the quantity and quality of snow in ski resorts. As the autumn progresses, snow falls at lower and lower altitudes, and this is announced in the weather bulletins every day. It is a sure sign that winter is on its way. Not long after, the announcements start giving the quantity of snow that has fallen in the various mountain ranges, and the French start to get out their skis!

🔊 KEYWORDS

le soleil	sun
la pluie	rain
la neige	snow
le vent	wind
le brouillard	fog
la gelée blanche	white frost
le beau temps	good weather
le mauvais temps	bad weather
Il fait froid.	It's cold.
Il fait chaud.	It's hot.
le bulletin météo	weather forecast
aller bien	to be well
avoir la pêche	to be on top of the world
être en pleine forme	to be feeling really well
être malade	to be ill
avoir un mal de tête	to have a headache
avoir mal à la gorge	to have a sore throat
avoir de la fièvre	to have a temperature
avoir la grippe	to have the flu
être enrhumé	to have a cold

La météo et la santé

CULTURAL TIPS

The various winds in France all have names. The most famous is *le mistral* that blows from the north down the Rhône valley to the sea. It clears the clouds from the sky, resulting in the famous blue Provençal skies, but is also cold. It is said to blow for either three, six or nine days.

French people contribute to complementary health insurance schemes to cover part or all of the difference between what the French public welfare system reimburses and the cost of any treatment. This insurance is called *une mutuelle* in reference to the mutual benefit organisations that run the schemes. Usually, when paying at the doctor or dentist for example, you are asked if you have *une mutuelle* and are given a bill that you then forward to the organisation you have chosen.

When French people have a heavy cold, they say, *"J'ai la crève." Crever* is a verb also meaning to die! However, when someone says, *"Je suis crevé,"* it just means they are very tired.

The French also pay great attention to their health. Some might even say they can be hypochondriacs! In French towns, *les pharmacies* usually have key locations and impressive window displays. Laboratories for analysing blood and urine samples abound and doctors' nameplates are numerous. The French visit their doctors frequently and are usually given prescriptions for several medicines at a time. French people are among the world's highest consumers of drugs, particularly where sleeping tablets and anti-depressants are concerned. It is therefore not surprising that, when the French meet each other, respective illnesses are subjects that are eagerly discussed.

So don't be surprised if, when talking to a French person, the conversation requires an understanding of some basic vocabulary about the weather and aches and pains!

FRENCH PEOPLE ARE VERY CONCERNED IF THE WEATHER ISN'T AS IT SHOULD BE FOR A GIVEN TIME OF YEAR.

La météo et la santé

HISTORY AND TRADITIONS

Weather bulletins on television in France usually end in a unique way. In the past, first names of French children had to be chosen from among the names listed on the calendar of saints or the administrative officer registering the birth wouldn't accept the name. Everyone therefore celebrated not only their birthday but also the day that corresponded to the saint's name on the calendar.

Weather updates usually conclude by giving the name of the saint associated with the next day as a reminder to wish people with that name a 'happy name day'. The naming rule was relaxed in 1966 when the list was enlarged to include the names of mythic characters and regional names.

In 1981, things were broadened further so most names, within reason, were allowed. Finally in 1993 the law was modified to allow virtually any first name, however many French people still have a saint's name as a first name.

🔊 USEFUL PHRASES

– Qu'est-ce qu'il fait beau !
   What lovely weather!
– Quel temps !
   What weather!
– Il fait très chaud aujourd'hui, n'est-ce pas ?
   It's very warm today, isn't it?
– Il a fait très froid hier.
   It was very cold yesterday.
– On apprécie ce beau temps, n'est-ce pas ?
   This good weather is really pleasant, isn't it?
– Comment allez-vous ?
   How are you?
– Vous avez bonne mine. _looking good_
   You're looking well.
– Je vais très bien, merci.
   I'm fine, thank you.
– Je suis en pleine forme.
   I'm feeling really well.
– Je suis un peu fatigué.
   I'm a bit tired.

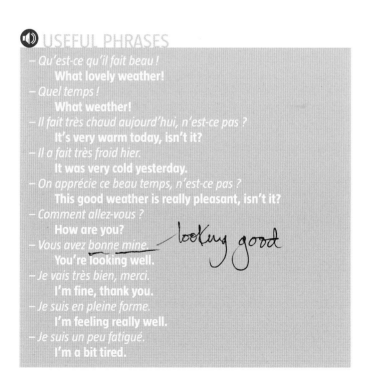

🔊 IDIOMS

– Il pleut des cordes means it's raining cats and dogs.
– Il fait un vent à décorner les bœufs means it's blowing a gale.
– Il fait un temps de chien means the weather is awful.
– Il n'est pas dans son assiette means he's feeling under the weather.

La météo et la santé

CULTURAL TIPS

Every French person has a green plastic smart card resembling a credit card. It's called *la carte vitale*. It allows the bearer to be identified and testifies to his reimbursement rights. Doctors and medical professionals use the card to communicate electronically with a central system and to pass on the details of their bills. Any reimbursements due are then paid directly into the bearer's bank account.

Every year, French people over the age of 60 and babies between the ages of six months and 23 months can be vaccinated for free to protect them from *la grippe*, the annual flu epidemic.

Some illnesses in France don't affect the body in the same places as in other countries! If you are nauseous, you will need to tell a French doctor that your heart is hurting: *"J'ai mal au cœur."* If you have an upset stomach, you will need to say that it's your liver: *"J'ai une crise de foie."* And if you have backache, it's your kidneys: *"J'ai mal aux reins."*

[handwritten: I have a liver crisis]

[handwritten: My kidneys hurt]

Every French child has a book containing his or her medical records. This is known as *le carnet de santé* and it records a child's medical history. It has been obligatory since 1942 and is given free at the child's birth. It is confidential and can be consulted, with the parents' agreement, by medical professionals only. Parents must give it to the family doctor during a visit and the doctor will keep a record of vaccinations in it as well as other medical details. It is no longer required when the child reaches the age of 16.

🔊 YOU WILL HEAR

— *Je trouve qu'il fait trop chaud, pas vous ?*
I find it too hot, don't you?
— *Je n'aime pas ce temps froid.*
I don't like this cold weather.
— *J'en ai marre de cette pluie.*
I'm fed up with this rain.
— *Il va faire meilleur la semaine prochaine.*
It's going to be better next week.
— *J'ai la pêche.*
I'm feeling on top of the world.
— *Pas trop mal. Et vous ?*
Not too bad. And you?
— *On fait aller.*
So-so.
— *Ce n'est pas la grande forme.*
I'm not feeling too well.

La météo et la santé

 LANGUAGE TIPS

When talking about the weather and health, there are two very useful verbs in French. For everything to do with the weather, the verb *faire* plus an adjective will help you say a lot:

– *Il fait gris.*
It's grey.

– *Il fait chaud.*
It's hot.

– *Il fait frais.*
It's cool.

If you have a health problem and need to visit a doctor, in many cases you can explain the problem by using the verb *avoir* and adding on the name of the part of the body concerned. This means you can simply say:

– *J'ai mal à l'épaule.*
My shoulder hurts.

– *J'ai mal au pied.*
My foot hurts.

 Remember

When French people are talking about *le temps* in French, they may not always be talking about the weather. The same word also means 'time', as in:
– *Je n'ai pas le temps.*
I haven't got the time.

Usually the context makes it quite clear which meaning is the appropriate one.

Remember that, when giving the temperature on a particular day, the French use the Celsius system. This also applies to body temperature. The normal body temperature is 37°C. However, when saying that somebody has a temperature, it is normal to say:
– *Il a de la fièvre.*

 ADVANCED USEFUL PHRASES

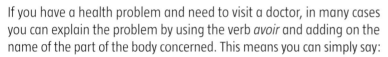

– *Quel mois de juillet pourri, n'est-ce pas ?*
What a rotten month of July, isn't it?
– *Vous avez quel temps en ce moment ?*
What's the weather like at the moment?
– *Ça s'est refroidi. Vous ne trouvez pas ?*
It's become colder. Don't you think?
– *Quel temps magnifique aujourd'hui ! On se croirait en plein été.*
What lovely weather today. It's just like summer.
– *Vous avez l'air en pleine forme.*
You're looking very well.
– *Vous avez été malade, je crois ?*
You've been ill, haven't you?
– *J'ai été un peu malade, mais ça va mieux maintenant.*
I wasn't very well, but I'm better now.
– *J'espère que vous allez bientôt vous sentir mieux.*
I hope you'll be better soon.

 **LEARN MORE**

You can refer to *Le dîner*, p.15, for other suggestions on starting a conversation.

For other examples of polite expressions you can use when meeting people, you can refer to *Les rencontres formelles*, p.38.

La météo et la santé

Most famous

La canicule is a heat wave. In August 2003, there was an exceptionally long-lasting heat wave that caused a substantial increase in the number of deaths during the period, particularly among older people. About 15,000 people are thought to have died as a result of the excessive heat. Since then, measures for improving the care of the elderly during a heat wave have been introduced. As soon as a new heat wave occurs, there are alerts on the television and advice given as to what to do to avoid problems. People are also requested to check on elderly neighbours.

A period of hot weather is classified as a heat wave in France if the difference between daytime and nighttime temperatures diminishes and the daytime temperature remains high for a period of 72 hours or more. In the south of France, this means when daytime temperatures are 35° C or higher and nighttime temperatures don't drop below 20° C. In the north, the temperatures are 30° C and 18° C respectively.

Quiz

It's a dogs time

Match the first half of the sentence with its second half.

A. J'ai mal... 3
B. Il fait... 4
C. Je suis... 2
D. Le temps va... 5
E. J'ai de... 6
F. J'en ai... 1

1. marre de la pluie.
✓ **2.** en pleine forme.
✓ **3.** au dos.
4. un temps de chien.
✓ **5.** se refroidir demain.
6. la fièvre.

Answers: A3, B4, C2, D5, E6, F1.

KEY POINTS

La météo et la santé...

- are two preferred topics of conversation.
- are prominent subjects on French television.
- are linked to economic concerns.
- reflect aspects of the French character and lifestyle.
- are conversational topics where you can cope with just a few keywords and two verbs.

La politique

WHAT TO EXPECT

The French love to discuss and even more to argue. Around a dinner table, in a *café*, at the local market, there will often be lively debates about current political issues. Don't be surprised if these discussions seem very heated. Gesticulating, raising voices and much contradicting are all part of the enjoyment.

From an early age, the school system teaches French children to debate and deal with abstract ideas. In the final year at school, many students study philosophy and final examinations include the writing of a dissertation in response to a philosophical question. The topics are even relayed on the television news programmes

and in the newspapers once the exam is over. People want to know what the questions were for that year. It's not surprising, therefore, that a love of debate is part of the national culture.

This inclination to express an opinion on current issues can be seen throughout French society. The plumber may be there to repair a burst pipe, but given a chance, he will tell you what he thinks of the taxes he pays, the government's policies and what needs to be changed. Your local shopkeeper will discuss changes in the country's economic situation or suggest the policies that Europe should adopt.

LE SÉNAT SITS AT THE *PALAIS DE LUXEMBOURG.*

CULTURAL TIPS

When exchanging viewpoints, you may be surprised to hear French people use the imperative form of verbs as if giving orders. In fact, although *écoutez* literally means 'listen', it is used more as a way of signalling to people that you are going to respond and tell them something. It is not insulting in any way.

The French often refer to ministers and their ministries by the names of the buildings they occupy. Hence *Matignon* becomes a substitute for the prime minister, *Bercy* for the Ministry of Finances, *Orsay* for the Ministry of Foreign Affairs and *Place Beauvau* for the Ministry of the Interior or Home Office. *L'Élysée* is of course synonymous with the French president.

La politique

Your neighbour will have fixed ideas on the education system. Everybody has an opinion and will not miss an opportunity to express it.

Intellectuals are, of course, highly thought of in France. To say that somebody is *intello* is not a criticism. Debates on political and social questions are held in prime time on television, especially when there are elections. Essays on social or philosophical questions are given prominence in bookstores, particularly when written by a well-known thinker or politician. Culture is taken very seriously.

POLITICAL DEBATE OVERFLOWS ONTO THE STREETS IN DEMONSTRATIONS AND PROTESTS.

CULTURAL TIPS

L'Assemblée nationale is the lower house of the French Parliament. Members are elected for five-year terms by universal suffrage and sit in a semicircular amphitheatre known as *l'Hémicycle* in the *Palais Bourbon* in Paris. *Le Sénat* is the upper house and sits at the *Palais de Luxembourg* in Paris. One-third of the members of the *Sénat* are elected for nine-year terms every three years by members of the lower house and other electoral representatives.

Important speeches by French politicians will start with an appeal to the French, *"Françaises, Français,"* and will finish with a rallying *"Vive la République ! Vive la France !"*

The French elect their president by universal suffrage. There are usually several candidates from the many different political parties. From the opening of the official election campaign, each candidate must be given equal time on television, even when the candidate only represents a very small political group.

La politique

This intellectual training and approach, the natural way that French people deal with abstract concepts, is combined with a preference for expressing their viewpoints forcefully. Compromise is not necessarily seen as a value. Political debate does not remain a simple exchange of ideas. It overflows onto the streets in demonstrations and protests. Prominent political figures march alongside protesters, debates on television can become noisy exchanges and your plumber will not hesitate, should you express a view contrary to his, to tell you bluntly that you are wrong, although he will take the time to explain why.

Guests who forcefully express differing opinions can make discussions around dinner tables somewhat overwhelming. This is especially true for people from cultures where politics or social questions are not discussed and where expressing contrary viewpoints can be considered bad manners. The French, however, will thoroughly enjoy such exchanges and will feel that they have had an opportunity to have their say. They will leave, voicing their appreciation of the evening and, of course, will not forget to thank their hosts for that other great topic of dinner conversation: the food.

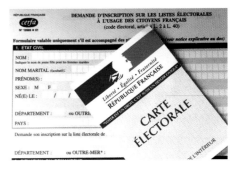

L'ASSEMBLÉE NATIONALE SITS IN THE *PALAIS BOURBON* IN PARIS.

🔊 KEYWORDS

la gauche	the left
la droite	the right
le président	president
le Premier ministre	prime minister
le maire	mayor
un parti politique	political party
une loi	law
un fonctionnaire	civil servant
un syndicat	union
une grève	strike
une manifestation	demonstration
inacceptable	unacceptable
inadmissible	intolerable
à mon avis	in my opinion
avoir raison	to be right
avoir tort	to be wrong
discuter	to discuss
débattre	to discuss

La politique

HISTORY AND TRADITIONS

The President of the French Republic used to be elected for a period of seven years, *un septennat*. In 2000, a proposition by a former president, Valéry Giscard d'Estaing, which was supported by the president at the time, Jacques Chirac, led to a constitutional referendum and the term was reduced to five years, *un quinquennat*. In 2008, a further revision of the constitution reduced the number of consecutive mandates a president could undertake to two. Previously, the number of mandates for a president under the *Cinquième République* had been unlimited.

French presidents are elected by direct universal suffrage. To win, a candidate must obtain an absolute majority, that is 50% of all votes cast plus one vote. As there are always several candidates, no candidate has ever obtained more than 50% in the first round.

CULTURAL TIPS

La rentrée is a busy period when French people return to work and children to school after the summer vacation. This term also refers to *la rentrée politique*, when the French Parliament reconvenes. It is often followed by a period of demonstrations and protests as new laws and political measures are proposed.

When a French person talks about *les infos*, they are referring to the television news broadcasts, an important part of the evening television programmes.

State employees and civil servants, *les fonctionnaires*, are often decried by the French, although they represent a significant proportion of the population. They are generally stereotyped and thought to have an easy life because of their job security. French people will often express their frustration with them as if they were responsible for everything that doesn't function properly in the country.

THE FRENCH OFTEN REFER TO MINISTERS AND THEIR MINISTRIES BY THE NAMES OF THE BUILDINGS THEY OCCUPY. HENCE *MATIGNON* BECOMES A SUBSTITUTE FOR THE PRIME MINISTER.

La politique

Consequently, a second vote takes place two weeks later when only the two candidates who obtained the most votes in the first round are on the ballot. The candidate who obtains a simple majority is elected.

French women won the right to vote in 1944 and voted for the first time in the local elections of 1945. All French citizens who are 18 and over and who have registered on the electoral role before December 31st can vote in any elections held the following year. There is no need to register again in following years unless the voter changes *communes*, the administrative district.

IDIOMS

- *La langue de bois* is waffle or talking without saying anything useful.
- *C'est la politique de l'autruche* means it's like burying one's head in the sand.
- *Une grève sauvage* is a wildcat strike, *une grève du zèle* is a work-to-rule and *une grève surprise* is a lightning strike.
- *Discuter le bout de gras* is to chat or argue away.

USEFUL PHRASES

– *La politique vous intéresse ?*
Does politics interest you?
– *Vous suivez la politique ?*
Do you keep up with politics?
– *Qu'est-ce que vous en pensez ?*
What do you think about it?
– *À votre avis, cette loi est-elle une bonne idée ?*
In your opinion, is this law a good idea?
– *Quel est l'intérêt de cette loi ?*
What is the point of this law?
– *Pourquoi y a-t-il une grève ?*
Why is there a strike?
– *Vous croyez que ça peut changer quelque chose ?*
Do you think it will change anything?
– *De qui parlez-vous ?*
Who are you talking about?
– *Quel est son rôle dans le gouvernement ?*
What is his role in the government?
– *Je n'arrive pas à suivre. Vous parlez un peu trop vite pour moi.*
I'm not following. You're talking a little too fast for me.
– *Je ne connais pas grande chose sur la politique française.*
I don't know much about French politics.

Remember

If you hear French people referring to somebody as a *député*, it means he or she is a member of the French Parliament, *l'Assemblée nationale*, not a deputy of any kind. That would be *un adjoint*.

Similarly, a *député-maire* is a member of Parliament who is also a mayor, although there is now a policy of dissuading people from holding more than one political office at a time. The *cumul des mandats* is strongly decried by many, but some politicians with more than one mandate are still reluctant to abandon one of them.

La politique

🔊 LANGUAGE TIPS

If the French people you are with start to discuss politics, it's probably best to observe rather than participate, unless you are very up-to-date with what is happening in France and very at ease in French. When people are involved in heated conversations they tend to speak quickly, making it more difficult to intervene appropriately. It is still possible to get the gist of the conversation as there are generally names and places, which will help you recognise what the conversation is about. You can also prepare by looking at French newspapers.

However, if your neighbour at the table starts to talk about political issues with you directly, you can take the opportunity to ask questions to continue the conversation even if you don't fully understand all the answers. If you are really lost, you can always say:
– *Je m'excuse, je ne comprends pas.*
I'm sorry, I don't understand.

– *Je suis désolé, je ne suis pas très au courant de ce sujet.*
I'm sorry, I don't know very much about this subject.

🔊 YOU WILL HEAR

– *Qu'est-ce que tu veux ?*
What do you expect?
– *Ce n'est pas admissible.*
It's not tolerable.
– *C'est de la folie.*
It's crazy.
– *Ce n'est pas normal.*
It's not right.
– *Je ne suis pas d'accord.*
I disagree.
– *À mon avis ça ne marchera pas.*
In my opinion, it won't work.
– *Il faut que ça s'arrête.*
It's got to stop.
– *Ça n'a pas de sens.*
It doesn't make sense.
– *Je suis complètement d'accord.*
I agree completely.
– *C'est exactement ça.*
That's exactly it.

 LEARN MORE

You can refer to *La famille,* p.52,
for other examples of asking questions.

For further examples of asking for explanations,
you can refer to *Les rencontres informelles,* p.45.

La politique

Most famous

Some of the most spectacular street protests in France took place during the student riots and general strike in May 1968 when the cobbles from the streets were famously thrown at the police. One of the slogans of the protests was, appropriately, *"sous les pavés, la plage"*, literally, "under the paving stones there's a beach". This generation became associated not only with political protests but also with a certain hippie lifestyle and utopian ideals. Even today, some French people will claim they are *soixante-huitards*, or will be referred to as such, that is, participants in the protests of 1968.

Le Salon de l'Agriculture is a very important event in France. It brings together farmers and their prize animals in a nine-day exhibition in Paris. It is a 'must-visit' for politicians who need to be seen and photographed talking with farmers and caressing the animals or tasting the food products. The French still accord a special place to farmers as representatives of traditional aspects of French life and there are many votes to be earned on such occasions.

🔊 ADVANCED USEFUL PHRASES

– *Quand on parle de Bercy, ça veut dire quoi ?*
  When people talk about Bercy, what does that mean?
– *Qu'est-ce que vous pensez du cumul des mandats ?*
  What do you think about politicians holding more than one electoral office?
– *Qu'est-ce que vous pensez de cette grève ?*
  What do you think about this strike?
– *Quel est l'enjeu de cette élection ?*
  What is at stake in this election?
– *Pourquoi ces gens manifestent ?*
  Why are these people demonstrating?
– *Quel est votre avis sur ce sujet ?*
  What's your opinion on the subject?
– *Quelle est la politique de la France par rapport aux personnes âgées ?*
  What policies do the French have with regard to older people?
– *Qu'est-ce que les Français pensent sur cette question ?*
  What do the French think about this issue?
– *Quelle est la position de la gauche à ce sujet ?*
  What is the position of the left on this issue?
– *Qu'est-ce que la droite propose ?*
  What does the right propose?

Quiz

Are the following statements true or false?

A. French presidents are elected for seven-year terms.
  ☐ True   ☑ False

B. The French avoid talking about politics.
  ☐ True   ☑ False

C. The Ministry of Finance can be referred to as *Bercy*.
  ☑ True   ☐ False

D. *Le Sénat* is the upper house of the French Parliament.
  ☑ True   ☐ False

E. French citizens have to be 21 to be able to vote.
  ☐ True   ☑ False

F. Intellectuals are respected in France.
  ☑ True   ☐ False

Answers: A. False, B. False, C. True, D. True, E. False, F. True.

KEY POINTS

La politique...

● is the subject of many conversations around dinner tables or in *cafés*.
● can lead to very heated debates.
● is a popular subject for television programmes and literary essays.
● can result in protests and demonstrations in the streets.
● is part of the culturally important *rentrée* in September.

La vie de tous les jours

WHAT TO EXPECT

You meet a French acquaintance in the street. You exchange comments on the weather and ask about each other's health. You enquire about the person's family. Your French friend kindly suggests you have a coffee in a nearby *café*. You choose a table and order your drink and then comes the moment you've been dreading. You need to make small talk in French for the next half hour or so. What can you say?

Everyday life, *la vie de tous les jours*, is a vast subject with lots of possibilities, but it is also more unpredictable and therefore more difficult to prepare. The more you know about the other person

the easier it will be and you will, of course, be able to rely on your French friend introducing topics of conversation. However, in a language in which you're not completely at ease, it's often simpler if you take the initiative. That way you can choose subjects that are easier for you and where you have more vocabulary.

CULTURAL TIPS

French people often use English words in everyday conversations, particularly when talking about computers and new technologies. You may not always recognise these words when pronounced with a French accent. Sometimes they will be slightly different from the English word, such as the use of *un mail* for an email. In French-speaking Quebec, an email is *un courriel*, but this word has never really caught on in France.

It may seem improbable, but if you use the wrong gender with a French word, French people will often not recognise the word. Also some words change meaning when the gender changes so it is important, when you learn a new word, to learn its gender at the same time.

IN A MORE INFORMAL CONVERSATION, YOU WILL FIND FRENCH PEOPLE USING MORE SLANG, IDIOMATIC EXPRESSIONS AND ABBREVIATED WORDS.

La vie de tous les jours

Asking lots of questions is also a good strategy. A straightforward enquiry about your French friend's work or leisure activity can result in lengthy descriptions or the recounting of recent events. Just be ready with a few encouraging words and nods to keep the conversation flowing. You may not follow everything they say, but as long as you get the gist, that will be sufficient.

A French person will almost certainly be interested in discovering aspects of your life also. When you talk about yourself, try to remember that it's important to say what you can and not what you would like to say. It will be difficult for the French person to maintain interest in what you are saying if you spend a lot of time searching for the right word, or enter into an elaborate explanation for which you don't have the structures. The simpler you keep it, the more natural the conversation will be.

🔊 KEYWORDS

la publicité	advertising, advertisement
le foot	football/soccer
le Tour	le Tour de France (cycle race)
le ski	skiing
un magazine	magazine
un livre	book
un roman	novel
une bande dessinée	comic album/book
un film	film
un mail	email
pratiquer un sport	to play a sport
les vacances	holidays/vacations
le bureau	office
la voiture	car
regarder la télé	to watch TV
faire les courses	to go shopping
jardiner	to garden
lire le journal	to read the newspaper
aller au cinéma	to go to the cinema/movies
envoyer un texto	to send an SMS text message

La vie de tous les jours

You will particularly please your French acquaintance if you express your interest in the local region and can say positive things about what you have found there. The French are always very proud of their region and will be delighted by this topic. Asking for recommendations of what to do and see or where to eat is a sure way of encouraging a local person to talk. Most French people will also be well-informed about the history and cultural aspects of their town or region and will be all too happy to give you plenty of information.

As long as you do not worry about understanding every word, or about making mistakes when you speak, you will find that the conversation boosts your confidence and that next time, maybe when you are sitting next to a French person at a dinner table, you will be delighted to have another opportunity to make small talk.

CULTURAL TIPS

When talking about their job, a French person will often say *mon job* instead of using the correct French term *mon travail*, although the slang *mon boulot* exists, too. You will also hear people talking about *le boss, une check-list, customiser* and *le brainstorming*. Sometimes the French word will be an adaptation of the English word, such as *le marketing, le planning* or *le reporting*.

The French enjoy sporting activities and will be happy to talk about them. If you don't know a word, it is often worth trying an English word. Many English words are used in connection with sports, so you will easily recognise *un penalty, un corner* or *shooter* when it comes to football (soccer) or *le caddie, un tee* and *le green* when it comes to golf.

When talking about events reported in the newspaper, French people will often refer to something that has *fait la une*, made the front pages or the headlines.

ASKING FOR RECOMMENDATIONS OF WHAT TO DO AND SEE OR WHERE TO EAT IS A SURE WAY OF ENCOURAGING A LOCAL PERSON TO TALK.

La vie de tous les jours

HISTORY AND TRADITIONS

The French have made great efforts over the centuries to protect the French language. More recently they have tried to ensure that it thrives despite the predominance of English.

L'Académie française was created by Cardinal Richelieu in 1635. Its mission was to codify the French language and to make it pure and eloquent. The Académie's first dictionary was published in 1694. At first, the Académie convened at the house of one or the other of its members, then at the Louvre and finally at the former *Collège des Quatre-Nations*, now known as the *Palais de l'Institut*, where it still meets today, once a week on Thursdays.

🔊 USEFUL PHRASES

– *Comment va votre jardin ?*
  How's your garden doing?
– *Vous avez passé de bonnes vacances ?*
  Did you have a good holiday/vacation?
– *Vous avez aimé ce livre ?*
  Did you like this book?
– *Vous avez vu le foot à la télé hier ?*
  Did you watch the football (soccer) match on television yesterday?
– *Vous avez reçu mon mail ?*
  Did you get my email?
– *Vous suivez le Tour ?*
  Do you follow the Tour de France?
– *Vous regardez beaucoup la télé ?*
  Do you watch a lot of television?
– *Vous partez souvent en week-end ?*
  Do you often go away for the weekend?
– *Vous rentrez tard du bureau ?*
  Do you get back late from the office?
– *Où est-ce que vous faites vos courses ?*
  Where do you do your shopping?

🔊 IDIOMS

– *Nous espérons vous lire bientôt* means we hope to hear from you soon.
– *C'est mon jardin secret* means I keep it very much to myself.
– *Parler de la pluie et du beau temps* means to talk about nothing in particular.
– *Parler à tort et à travers* is to talk through one's hat or wildly.

La vie de tous les jours

CULTURAL TIPS

Difficulties linked to transport are a frequent topic of conversation. People living in or near Paris often have long and difficult journeys to and from work. Rush hour, *l'heure de pointe*, is around 8 o'clock in the morning and between 6 and 7 o'clock in the evening. Traffic is usually dense at these times and traffic jams, *les bouchons*, are frequent. Journeys on the *métro* can be long, and the famous phrase, *"métro, boulot, dodo"* – commute, work, sleep – is said to sum up the life of many Parisians.

The French are proud of their cinema and it is part of what is known as *l'exception culturelle*. In order to protect the French cinema and maintain cultural diversity, French television channels are required to invest a percentage of their annual turnover in French cinema productions. They must also ensure that at least 40% of their broadcasts are French productions.

The members of the Académie française are known as *Les immortels*, a reference to the motto *"À l'immortalité"*, which was inscribed on the seal given to the Académie by Richelieu, thus proclaiming its mission to preserve the French language. There are a maximum of 40 *Immortels* at any one time, and once elected, they hold office for life. The Académie itself elects new members once a seat becomes vacant, although the French president must approve of the appointment.

Among former *Immortels* are Pierre Corneille, Jean de La Fontaine, Victor Hugo, Voltaire, Louis Pasteur and Léopold Senghor. Émile Zola failed to get himself elected, even though he tried on 25 occasions.

Although the Académie is an official authority on the French language, particularly on questions of grammar, vocabulary and usage, its rulings are not binding.

THE MISSION OF THE ACADÉMIE FRANÇAISE IS TO CODIFY THE FRENCH LANGUAGE AND TO MAKE IT PURE AND ELOQUENT.

🔊 YOU WILL HEAR

– *Qu'est-ce que vous avez fait aujourd'hui ?*
What did you do today?
– *Qu'est-ce que vous pensez de la région ?*
What do you think of the region?
– *Vous marchez beaucoup ?*
Do you walk a lot?
– *Vous êtes allé au marché ?*
Have you been to the market?
– *C'est la course. Je n'arrête pas.*
It's a race against the clock. I never stop.
– *J'ai passé samedi à tondre la pelouse.*
I spent Saturday mowing the lawn.
– *Je suis allé voir des amis à Nice ce week-end.*
I went to see some friends in Nice this weekend.
– *Je m'effondre devant la télé le soir.*
I collapse in front of the TV in the evenings.

La vie de tous les jours

🔊 LANGUAGE TIPS

When chatting with French people, it's useful to have a few phrases to express your interest in what they are saying. You can use phrases such as:

– Ça, c'est bon à savoir.
That's useful to know.

– Ça, c'est intéressant.
That's interesting.

You may also want to express surprise at something they say, in which case you can say:

– C'est pas vrai !
I don't believe it!

– Sans blague ?
Really?

– J'en reviens pas.
I can't get over it.

When you want to express approval, you can say:

– C'est génial !
That's great!

– Super !
Fantastic!

To express agreement,
you can say:

– Exactement!
Exactly!

– Je suis complètement d'accord.
I agree completely.

🔊 *Remember*

When talking with French people about everyday life, don't forget to observe the necessary degree of formality. As always, you should follow the French person's lead and avoid questions that might be considered intrusive if the contact is very formal.

In a more informal conversation, you will find French people using more slang, idiomatic expressions and abbreviated words. This can make a conversation more difficult to follow, so it's worth knowing some of the more current slang words even if you don't use them yourself. Otherwise, when you hear people talking about *le cinoche, un resto* or *la fac*, you may not understand that they are referring to the cinema, a restaurant or the university.

You can, of course, always request an explanation by asking:
– Ça veut dire quoi 'le cinoche' ?
What does *'cinoche'* mean?

 **LEARN MORE**

You can find other examples of informal language in *Les rencontres informelles*, p.45.

For other examples of asking questions, you can refer to *La politique*, p.75.

La vie de tous les jours

Most famous

Literary salons organised by women were extremely popular in the 17th century and continued into the 19th century. Aristocratic women invited the intellectuals of the time, both men and women, to discuss a variety of topics. Many also maintained an abundant correspondence, the most famous of which are the letters of Madame de Sévigné. It was in these salons that the French art of conversation was developed.

One of the last great salons was that of Virginie Ancelot who, right up until her death in 1875, welcomed into her salon the prominent thinkers of the day. Among the famous writers who attended were Victor Hugo, Alphonse Daudet, Stendhal and Alphonse de Lamartine.

you take care

Quiz

Fill in the blanks using the word bank below.
bureau, courses, vacances, jardin, roman, télé
C F E a b d

A. *Vous vous occupez beaucoup de votre* _____ ?

B. *Vous avez lu ce* _____ ?

C. *À quelle heure vous rentrez du* _____ *le soir ?*

D. *Je regarde beaucoup la* _____ *le soir.*

E. *Vous avez passé de bonnes* _____ ?

F. *Où est-ce que vous faites vos* _____ ?

Answers: A. *jardin*, B. *roman*, C. *bureau*, D. *télé*, E. *vacances*, F. *courses.*

🔊 ADVANCED USEFUL PHRASES

– *Je passe beaucoup de temps dans mon jardin.*
I spend a lot of time in my garden.
– *J'adore faire le tour des marchés locaux.*
I love going around the local markets.
– *J'essaie de lire des romans en français.*
I'm trying to read some novels in French.
– *Je travaille beaucoup, donc j'apprécie d'avoir un peu de temps libre.*
I work a lot, so I appreciate having some free time.
– *Vos enfants vont-ils à l'école du village ?*
Do your children go to the school in the village?
– *Vous travaillez dans une agence de publicité, je crois ?*
You work in an advertising agency, don't you?
– *Votre famille est dans la région ?*
Does your family live nearby?
– *Vous partez au ski ce dimanche ?*
Are you going skiing on Sunday?

KEY POINTS

La vie de tous les jours...

● is an unpredictable topic of conversation.
● is a common subject for small talk.
● is a topic requiring some knowledge of slang.
● is a topic where you need to prepare some information about yourself.
● is a topic where you should take the initiative when possible.

L'humour

WHAT TO EXPECT

Go into any book shop in France and it is likely you will see several adults propped against the shelves or even sitting on the floor reading. What is keeping them so engrossed? You may be surprised if you draw closer to have a look. They will quite probably be reading a comic album. Children's books, you may catch yourself thinking. Not in France — or at least not exclusively.

The fascination with comic albums has existed for many years and many adults will talk about their collections with pride. They will discuss the work of their preferred authors, the quality of the drawings, the differences between authors and the merits of their favourite volumes. Ask your French neighbour at the table about their preferred comic album author and you will have started a passionate conversation!

French humour is different in other ways, too. Say something a little tongue-in-cheek and you may find to your embarrassment that what you have said is taken literally. The first reaction of a French person is to assume you are speaking seriously. Trying to backtrack out of a well-intentioned amusing comment can be tricky, especially in French!

CULTURAL TIPS

French politicians are mocked in television programmes such as 'Les Guignols de l'Info,' or 'news puppets', which is the French equivalent of the British programme 'Spitting Image'. Le Canard Enchaîné, a satirical newspaper famous for its investigative journalism and its independence, has been published since 1915 and specialises in reporting, often humorously, on political scandals.

The French cartoonist known as Plantu specialises in political satire. He has a regular cartoon on a political or topical issue on the front page of Le Monde, a highbrow daily French newspaper. His trademark is a little mouse, which is always hidden somewhere in the cartoon and acts as a further humorous comment on the subject matter.

L'humour

CULTURAL TIPS

Many nationalities select another nation as the butt of their jokes. For the French it is the Belgians whom they consider as not very bright, and numerous Belgian jokes abound. There are also many jokes about Corsicans, who are portrayed as being abnormally slow.

The French make noises with their mouths, roll their eyes, shrug and gesture a lot when they are talking, and French comedians exaggerate this habit in their sketches. Being able to recognise some of the common gestures is useful, although the context usually makes it clear. When with French people, it is probably best not to try to imitate these gestures, though!

Don't expect the French to use self-mockery, either. If they tell a story about something that has happened, it will usually be simply to give you the details, or to emphasise how difficult or awful a situation was, rather than to make you laugh by portraying themselves in an ironic or humorous light. They will seldom use a good story to make fun of themselves.

You're attending a conference in France? A businessman is making a presentation? Don't expect a joke or a humorous introduction.

L'humour

Why not? A French person would be worried that he might lose his credibility. It is important not to appear frivolous. François Hollande, as a presidential candidate in 2012, dramatically changed his image so that the French electorate would consider him a suitable president. Known as a jolly person ready to make jokes, he completely suppressed this aspect of his personality during the campaign. He became somebody the French would see as _sérieux_. Interestingly, in French, this word means reliable and dependable, vital characteristics for a presidential candidate.

Does all of this mean that the French have no sense of humour? Far from it. Their humour stretches from slapstick and farce to delicate wordplay or biting black humour. The French may refer to the English as speaking _la langue de Shakespeare_, but they will refer to themselves as speaking _la langue de Molière_, the 17th-century French playwright who wrote comedies and is considered one of the masters of the genre. So, if you are sitting around a French dinner table, there will still be laughter, just maybe not for the reasons you might expect.

 IDIOMS

- _Rire comme une baleine_ is to be doubled up with laughter.
- _C'est à mourir de rire_ means it's really hilarious.
- _Il vaut mieux en rire qu'en pleurer_ means it's better to look on the bright side.
- _Rira bien qui rira le dernier_ means he who laughs last laughs longest.

KEYWORDS

une blague	joke
un jeu de mots	pun
une anecdote	anecdote
une plaisanterie	joke
une histoire drôle	funny story
une farce	practical joke
un humoriste	humorist
l'humour noir	black humour
la grosse farce	slapstick comedy
drôle	funny
rigolo	funny
amusant	amusing
humoristique	humorous
sourire	to smile
rire	to laugh
rire aux éclats	to roar with laughter
rigoler	to laugh
plaisanter	to joke
se moquer de soi-même	to make fun of oneself
manquer d'humour	to have no sense of humour

L'humour

MOLIÈRE BECAME THE OFFICIAL AUTHOR OF COURT ENTERTAINMENT.

HISTORY AND TRADITIONS

Talk to a French person about French comedy and he or she will almost certainly refer to Molière. Jean-Baptiste Poquelin was born in 1622. After finishing his studies he became an actor and started, at the same time, to write plays. Aided by different patrons, Poquelin, under his stage name Molière, eventually performed in front of Louis XIV at the Louvre. The king granted Molière a pension for his troupe and he became the official author of court entertainment. His plays were performed at the Palais-Royal and were highly regarded by Parisians.

Among his most famous plays are 'L'École des femmes', 'Les Femmes savantes', 'L'Avare' and 'Tartuffe'. The latter's condemnation of religious hypocrisy brought much criticism from the Roman Catholic Church, but Molière kept the king's favour.

CULTURAL TIPS

When telling a joke or in comic sketches, slang is often used. This can make French humour a little difficult to understand for the foreigner. You can always ask for an explanation, but you will find that, little by little, you will become familiar with the most commonly used slang words.

You may hear French people saying they have watched a 'one-man show', using the English term. You may have difficulty recognising the words as the way it is pronounced in French makes it sound as if there is an 'h' at the beginning of the phrase.

If a French person has a fit of giggles, he or she is said to have *le fou rire*, literally crazy laughter.

🔊 USEFUL PHRASES

– *C'est très drôle.*
It's very funny.
– *C'est amusant.*
It's very amusing.
– *C'est une histoire drôle.*
It's a funny story.
– *C'est une très bonne blague.*
It's a very good joke.
– *Vous aimez raconter des blagues ?*
Do you like telling jokes?
– *Vous connaissez une bonne blague en français ?*
Do you know a good joke in French?
– *Vous aimez les films drôles ?*
Do you like comedy films?
– *Vous avez beaucoup d'humour.*
You have a good sense of humour.

L'humour

IF A FRENCH PERSON
HAS A FIT OF GIGGLES,
HE OR SHE IS SAID TO HAVE
LE FOU RIRE, LITERALLY
CRAZY LAUGHTER.

🔊 Remember

Some words referring to humour can be a bit tricky. *Un comédien* is an actor, not a comedian, and *une comédienne* is an actress. Note that you can also say *un acteur* and *une actrice*. You would need to say *un comédien comique* to mean a comic actor and *un comique* to mean a comedian, although *un humoriste* would be the term used generally.

La Comédie-Française is the historic theatre company in Paris that has a mainly classical repertoire.

When talking about humour in French, remember to pronounce it correctly. *L'humour* and *l'humeur* are very similar. The latter means mood or temperament, so if you say someone *est de mauvaise humeur*, it means the person is in a bad mood. It has nothing to do with the quality of the person's sense of humour!

huumoor *huumer*

🔊 YOU WILL HEAR

– *Elle n'est pas mal, celle-là.*
   That's a good one.
– *Je vais vous raconter quelque chose.* *gifted*
   I'm going to tell you something.
– *Je ne suis pas très doué pour raconter les blagues.* *douer – to endow*
   I'm not very good at telling jokes.
– *Vous avez un humour très British !*
   You have a very British sense of humour!
– *J'aime beaucoup les bandes dessinées.*
   I really like comic albums.
– *Je ne regarde pas beaucoup les émissions humoristiques.*
   I don't watch comedy programmes very much.
– *Vous connaissez des humoristes français ?*
   Do you know any French comedians?
– *J'ai lu quelque chose de très drôle dans le journal.*
   I read something very funny in the paper.

In 1673, after a period of poor health resulting from overwork, Molière suffered a haemorrhage while performing in one of his plays, 'Le Malade Imaginaire'. He completed the performance, but died a few hours later.

Molière was the creator of modern French comedy and his plays are still widely performed today. Even the names of some of his characters have made their way into the French language. *Un harpagon* is a very greedy man, as was the character named Harpagon in Molière's play 'L'Avare'. *Un tartuffe* is a hypocrite, the word coming from the play of the same name about a hypocrite named Tartuffe.

L'humour

Most famous

Raymond Devos was a famous Franco-Belgian stand-up comic who was very talented with wordplay. His sketches often revolved around the use and multiple meanings and associations of a particular word. He was also famous for taking a given word and modifying it gradually, each time maintaining a meaning, until it became another word entirely. He was recognised as a master of the French language.

Among famous French stand-up comics, one of the most respected is Guy Bedos. As well as being known for his many appearances in films, he has toured France for many years with a series of one-man shows. Particularly appreciated was 'la revue de presse', or the news coverage, which became his trademark. It consisted of a series of rapid, ironic and biting comments on topical and political events and was always a part of his shows.

🔊 LANGUAGE TIPS

Telling a joke in another language is very difficult, even when it doesn't rely on a pun for the punch line. It's best, therefore, to avoid trying to translate a joke you know into French. It can be a painful experience for both you and your listener!

However, you may well need to laugh appropriately at a French joke. If you haven't understood, you can say:
– *Je suis désolé, mais je n'ai pas compris.*
I'm sorry, but I didn't understand.

– *Vous pouvez répéter la blague ? Je n'ai pas compris la première fois.*
Can you say it again? I didn't understand the first time.

– *C'est un peu compliqué pour moi. Je suis désolé.*
It's a bit difficult for me. I'm sorry.

 **LEARN MORE**

You can refer to *La politique*, p.75, for other examples of asking questions.

There are further examples of asking for more information in *Les différences régionales*, p.59.

L'humour

ADVANCED USEFUL PHRASES

– *Quels sont les humoristes français les plus appréciés actuellement ?*
Who are the most popular French comedians at the moment?
– *Quelles sont les caractéristiques de l'humour français ?*
What are the characteristics of French humour?
– *Est-ce que vous aimez regarder des films humoristiques ?*
Do you like watching comedies?
– *Avez-vous une collection de bandes dessinées ?*
Do you collect comic albums?
– *Quel est votre auteur de bandes dessinées préféré ?*
Who is your favourite comic album author?
– *Est-ce que vous pensez que les Français ont beaucoup d'humour ?*
Do you think the French have a good sense of humour?
– *Qu'est-ce que vous pensez de l'humour British ?*
What do you think of the British sense of humour?
– *Vous aimez les films humoristiques américains ?*
Do you like American comedies?

Quiz

Are the following statements true or false?

A. In France, wordplays are much appreciated.
☑ True   ☐ False

B. Belgians are often the butt of French jokes.
☑ True   ☐ False

C. Plantu's trademark in his cartoon drawings is a little bird.
☐ True   ☑ False

D. Molière died during a performance in one of his own plays.
☐ True   ☑ False

E. Comic albums are very popular with French adults.
☑ True   ☐ False

F. When giving a presentation in France, it's a good idea to start with a joke.
☐ True   ☑ False

Answers: A. True, B. True, C. False, D. False, E. True, F. False.

KEY POINTS

L'humour...

- in France is not based on self-mockery.
- can involve a lot of wordplay.
- is not always considered suitable in serious contexts.
- is very different from British or American humour.
- can include elements of farce.

As they say in French

- « *L'humour est la politesse du désespoir.* »
  Georges Duhamel

- « *La météo est une science qui permet de connaître le temps qu'il aurait dû faire.* » *it should have done*
  Philippe Bouvard *Thereafter* *weapon*

- « *Quand vous êtes très jeune, l'humour est une défense. Par la suite, il peut devenir une arme.* »
  René Goscinny

- « *J'ai décidé d'être heureux parce que c'est bon pour la santé.* »
  Voltaire

  it's the preserve

- « *Le travail c'est la santé ; ne rien faire, c'est la conserver.* »
  Henri Salvador

Pam Bourgeois' name has long been associated with creative and effective language learning methods. Her techniques are based on years of experience running language schools for an international clientele and creating language-study materials in Europe and Africa. She has worked as a consultant in business French for the BBC and co-authored OBJECTIFS: ASSIGNMENTS IN PRACTICAL LANGUAGE SKILLS (Cambridge University Press).

Pam has lived and worked for over 25 years in France where she established language schools, created and was editor-in-chief of several language magazines and developed a series of over 30 audio learning guides in three languages.

Her expertise in language acquisition and passion for cultural understanding inspired her to create Kolibri Languages and publish a series of PRACTICAL GUIDES TO LIFESTYLE, MANNERS AND LANGUAGE. The guides highlight the importance of cultural awareness when learning a language or visiting another country.

Also available as a Kolibri Languages PRACTICAL GUIDE TO LIFESTYLE, MANNERS AND LANGUAGE

EATING AND SHOPPING IN FRANCE
Pam Bourgeois

In EATING AND SHOPPING IN FRANCE, you will discover everything you need to know to enable you to eat well and do your shopping in France. Cultural tips, historical anecdotes, useful words and expressions, amusing idioms, quizzes and key information will help you understand the French way of life.

- Discover the polite way to cut French cheeses.
- Learn why Marseille is associated with soap.
- Discover the differences between a Parisian brasserie and a 'bouchon' in Lyon.
- Learn key vocabulary for talking about wine.
- Prepare yourself for shopping in French markets with key information.
- Know what to expect when you go into traditional French food shops.

EATING AND SHOPPING IN FRANCE will help you prepare your trip and will be a unique souvenir when you return home.

ISBN : 979-10-91624-00-8

www.kolibrilanguages.com

© Pam Bourgeois, 2012
publié par Kolibri Languages (département de LinguaProduction sarl)
Les Meules, 69640 Cogny - France

MEETING THE FRENCH
ISBN : 979-10-91624-04-6

Dépôt légal : novembre 2012
Imprimé en France (Printed in France) novembre 2012
par Chevillon Imprimeur, 26 boulevard Kennedy, 89100 Sens